BOAT
IMPROVEMENTS
PRACTICAL
for the
SAILOR

BOAT
IMPROVEMENTS
PRACTICAL *for the* TICAL
SAILOR

STEPHEN J. FISHMAN

SHERIDAN HOUSE

First published 1999 by
Sheridan House Inc.
145 Palisade Street
Dobbs Ferry, NY 10522

Illustrations by author
Edited by Dianne Thomas, Providence Road Press
Designed by Collin R. Young, Providence Road Press

Library of Congress Cataloging-in-Publication Data

Fishman, Stephen J.
    Boat improvements for the practical sailor / Stephen J. Fishman.
        p.   cm.
    Includes index.
    ISBN 1-57409-068-2 (alk. paper)
    1. Boats and boating—Maintenance and repair.   I. Title.
VM322.F57   1999
623.8'3—dc21   99-19850
                                                                    CIP

Printed in the United States of America

This book is dedicated to my wife Deborah, whose confidence in my success quelled any nagging doubts I may have had about getting the book published.

I will love you, till time and tides are through.

ACKNOWLEDGMENTS

The list is short, but significant...

To the many clients whose sailboats and motoryachts were the proving ground for my theory that boat repairs are not a black art.

To the many marine contractors without whom many of these projects would have been more difficult to distill into plain English.

To Steve Bowden of Sea Tech Systems who first made me realize that there were more rewards to writing than just the byline.

And finally to Kay and Mike Dubois for their friendship and their willingness to provide an opportunity for my theory to be tested.

CONTENTS

INTRODUCTION

There are dozens of books written about the "craftsmanship" of boat repairs and upgrades. While most of these books provide valuable information for the boat owner, they seem to assume that the reader has access to an unlimited array of power and hand tools as well as the training and skill to use those tools well. In my experience, the typical boat owner has neither. Although many do-it-yourself authors are experts in their specialty, and rightly so, the typical boat owner is at best a jack of all trades and a craftsman in none. It is for these skippers — people like me — that I wrote this book.

Many of these chapters originally appeared as articles written for boat owner association newsletters or sailing magazines. My belief is this: If a guy like me — with average skills and common tools — can do this stuff, so can any other boat owner. Unquestionably, there are many repairs and upgrades best left to specialists, but there are *far more* that a typical boat owner can expect to be able to complete.

Like many others, I dreamed for years of owning a sailboat. Almost exactly eleven years to the day from my first sail, I bought a 1986 O'Day 28 sloop. She was four years old, and had been neglected in a slip for three of those years. From the very beginning, I was determined to restore the boat to its original condition — or better.

That was almost nine years ago: I was fairly bursting at the seams to install, modify and otherwise fix almost anything on my "new" boat. But the fact was, I had never installed, modified or otherwise fixed anything on *any* boat before!

Now I am not the world's best handyman, but reasoning that boat repairs couldn't be that much different from home improvements, I set about making my list of to-do's. The list was extensive, since the boat had been almost completely ignored for the better part of three years. To make matters worse, the prior owner had added nothing to the boat since the day it was launched — not even a name. This was a needy boat! The only extras already on board were a stereo radio with two cabin speakers and a rolling furling with a 150% genoa. And so I was presented with the opportunity (and expense) of adding or modifying almost anything in the way of hardware, electronics or appearance items.

I created two lists (1) things I thought I could accomplish myself, and (2) tasks I felt a professional should handle. With time, my confidence grew; I found the first list growing and the second list shrinking.

Our family christened the boat *Jenny Reb*, after my daughter Jennifer Rebecca, and placed the name proudly on the stern in eight-inch burgundy vinyl letters.

The first task was to develop a plan. After a bit of research, I began stocking a parts box and fastener bin. And once I understood the materials and techniques involved in accomplishing these projects, the necessary supplies became evident. Add to this the assortment of hand and power tools needed, and the basics were covered.

At the top of my list were several items that required specialized equipment, which I had no interest in doing myself — a replacement mailsail cover and wheel bag as well as a new bimini. These were also to be made in burgundy. Although canvas work can change the overall appearance of a boat more quickly than almost anything else, other things can also significantly affect a boat's appearance. I covered the blue stripes on the hull near the deck with 1½" and ½" burgundy vinyl stripes, and the change was immediate and significant. Later, I added a double pinstripe to the toerail, along with a set of cockpit cushions in a cream-colored seat with burgundy side panels. Color made an enormous difference.

Next came some minor repair items long overlooked on this boat. I removed the headsail from the roller furling so a local loft could repair the foot that had been damaged by chafing against lifeline turnbuckles. I rehung the folding door to the V-berth. Next, the check valve leading to the water heater had to be removed and reversed in order to allow water to flow into the heater. (It had been installed backwards at the factory.) Lack of use and age had taken their toll. The head needed a new set of gaskets. I'm sure you get the idea!

Then came the stuff that looked like nothing but *hard work*. The boat was in desperate need of a good compound and polish. This is recommended semi-annually, but in this case it hadn't been done for four years. If you've ever polished a boat, you know that this task is the one maintenance job guaranteed to convince anyone that bigger is not necessarily better. Well this was now my boat, and every square inch of smooth fiberglass above the waterline received this treatment.

Instead of waxes, I used industrial-strength cleaners on the non-skid portions of the deck so the surface could do what it was designed to do — provide a non-slip surface. What's more, all the lines were hard and stick-like; they required soaking in soap and water so they would bend enough to actually wrap a winch.

But everything was relative: Of all the cleanup chores, nothing was worse than scooping the slime out of the anchor locker... and neutralizing the alien life that had developed in the icebox. This was not boating — it was *work*! The only consolation was that this amount of dirt would never again be found on this boat. Indeed, these types of problems can be easily kept in check with regular light maintenance.

"There is always something to be done on a boat" — one of the Great Truths of the Universe.

It ranks right up there with the quote about the best days in a boat owner's life — the day he or she buys, and the day the boat is sold. Nonetheless, only a little over four years after I bought the boat, I was able to complete the entire to-do list! And the rewards were immediate: a few months after completing the list, my wife and I were presented with an offer for our sailboat. It was too good to pass up; we sold *Jenny Reb* and bought a larger boat, then moved on board permanently. It was all so quick: It seemed a shame to sell the boat so soon after completion, but we could not ignore the opportunity to move aboard. Now, almost five years later, we still find living aboard a *marvelous* lifestyle.

These five years have brought a great deal of joy, more experience, and repeated requests by slip neighbors to help with maintenance and upgrades. I've been encouraged to share my experiences and skills with other skippers, and this book is the next natural step. Happy upgrade!

SJF

Kemah, Texas
January 1999

Chapter One
The Nuts and Bolts of Nuts and Bolts

Whether your modification is electrical or mechanical, plumbing, carpentry or fiberglass, it has something in common with nearly all other upgrade or refit projects in that most use fasteners of some type. This chapter discusses these essential items.

Fasteners are a group of hardware items that are used to hold components or equipment together. A fastener can be a screw, a nut, a washer, a nail or a rivet. For canvas work, a fastener can be a twist fastener, a snap, a zipper, a button or a grommet. The specific item in question could be made from plastic, brass, bronze, stainless steel or almost any metal. The variety and sizes available can provide a precise match to virtually any purpose, provided that you understand the application. The context of this discussion will not be concerned with fasteners that are specific to canvas products, but rather those that are more generally used to hold one item to another. Let's begin with screws.

Screws

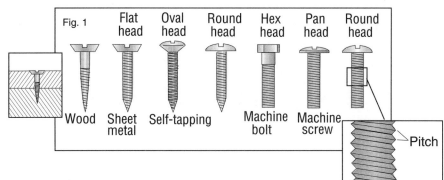

Fig. 1 — Flat head / Oval head / Round head / Hex head / Pan head / Round head; Wood / Sheet metal / Self-tapping / Machine bolt / Machine screw / Pitch

Athough screws (Fig. 1) are the most familiar category of fastener, there is often confusion as to which type is best for a specific purpose. However, before discussing applications, an understanding of the differences between types of screws is useful. Screws can be identified in as many as four ways:

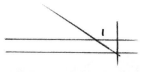

RULE of THUMB

Duct tape – although often used as a means to hold a wide variety of things together, it is not strictly a fastener. It was invented, and is still best used for, sealing plenums and ducts in air conditioning systems.

1. An even number from, four to fourteen, that refers to the thickness of the shank. The higher the number designation, the larger the diameter of the shank.
2. The measured length of the shank in inches. The higher the number of the measured length, the longer the shank.
3. The configuration of the head. The size of the head will always be proportionate to the diameter of the shank, and the shape of the head will help determine its suitability for a specific application.
4. In some cases, the pitch of the threads. The pitch refers to the number of threads per linear inch of the shank.

A **wood screw** is shown in Figure 1 and, as the name implies, is a fastener intended for use with wood only. A wood screw is identified by an even number from four to fourteen (#6, #8, etc.) that represents the diameter of the shank and a dimension, in inches, that indicates the shank length. Wood screws are most commonly found with a flat head. As an example of the description code, you might shop for a "1-inch #8 wood screw."

The threads on the shank of a wood screw do not extend the full length of the shank from point to head. Typically, the piece of wood on top is drilled completely through in a diameter larger than the fastener, while the piece on the bottom is drilled smaller than the fastener. A countersink is used to recess the head of the screw, rendering it flush with the surface of the wood.

Sheet metal screws are much more common than the wood variety. These fasteners have threads that run the entire length of the shank from point to head, and can be used to hold together wood, metal, plastics or fiberglass in any combination. Originally designed to hold two or more pieces of sheet metal together, sheet metal screws are used in applications in which either the fastener cannot be extended all the way through the component (i.e. a clock that has been installed on a bulkhead) or when the leading end of the screw cannot be reached once installed (a hull liner, for example).

Sheet metal screws are also identified by an even number

RULES of THUMB

Wood screws are less secure than other types of fasteners due to the lack of threads along the entire length of the shank and, as a result, are seldom used on boats.

Always drill a pilot hole that is smaller in diameter than the fastener. In wood, this means drilling a hole that is two sizes smaller; in fiberglass, only one size smaller. If the material is metal, the hole should not be merely a pilot hole but, instead, should match the shank of the fastener as closely as possible.

from four to fourteen (#6, #8, etc.). This number represents the diameter of the shank, while a dimension in inches indicates the shank length, and a shape specification describes the configuration of the head. An example of this description code might describe a fastener as follows: "1½-inch #8 oval head sheet metal screw."

This may sound like a mouthful, but it is the only way you can be assured of purchasing exactly what you intend to use.

When a sheet metal screw is used, the screw should be installed only after a pilot hole has been drilled. This will avoid splitting teak and other woods, or prevent twisting the head off the fastener when screwed forcibly into fiberglass. If you are attaching an item to a thick-walled metal such as a stainless steel pedestal guard or an aluminum boom, it is often possible to use a self-tapping sheet metal screw in order to achieve a more secure attachment.

Machine screws and **machine bolts** are types of fasteners without a point; the flat tip is meant to be completely inserted through a material. After insertion, these fasteners are held in place either with a washer and a nut on the end opposite the head, or by threads that have been tapped into the hole. These fasteners are identified with all four criteria — an even number, a measurement in inches, a head configuration and a specification for thread pitch.

Pitch refers to the number of threads per inch on the shank. An example of a machine screw or machine bolt description could be the following: "2-inch 10-24 round head machine screw." It is necessary to know the pitch in order to purchase a nut; the washer must match the diameter of the shank, but a nut must match the pitch of the threads.

Machine bolts are somewhat more specialized. Threaded only partway to the head, they are used primarily for engine components or installing major structural items such as pulpits and bowsprits. Machine screws, on the other hand, can be found in almost any application in which metal or plastic is joined, such as through-deck installations or fastening hardware to a mast or boom. *Note: Pop rivets are an option for many applications in which machine screws are appropriate, but I have always felt that machine screws are more secure than pop rivets.*

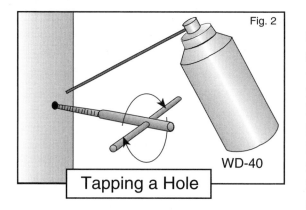

Fig. 2

WD-40

Tapping a Hole

It is also necessary to know the thread pitch of a machine screw if the hole is to be tapped (Fig. 2). A tap is used to create threads in a hole after it has been drilled, most commonly in metal. After selecting a tap tool to match the pitch of the machine screw, insert the tap into the hole and rotate clockwise. Spray a lubricant,

such as WD-40, onto the tap's cutting threads as well as into the hole; this will reduce heat and create threads that are cleaner and smoother. A substantial amount of heat is generated as the tap cuts the metal; lubricant will help prevent the tap from breaking off or seizing up in the hole.

When installing machine screws, use the shortest possible shank length in order to avoid interfering with unseen components such as lines and wiring. If a machine screw is installed into a threaded hole using a lock washer and Loctite, it will remain secure indefinitely.

One final comment on sheet metal screws: The style of the head can be flat, oval or round, the choice dependent upon the application and the desired appearance. For instance, a round head screw would look best against a flat surface such as the base of a stanchion, while an oval or flat head might be used for countersunk holes in eye straps or in wood.

Washers and nuts

Washers in their most common forms are shown Figure 3. Their purpose is:

- to help secure a nut when a screw is through-bolted,
- as a spacer beneath the head of a non-countersunk fastener, or
- both of the above.

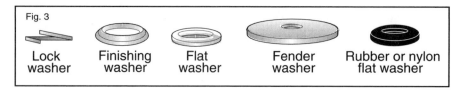

Fig. 3

| Lock washer | Finishing washer | Flat washer | Fender washer | Rubber or nylon flat washer |

Lock washers provide a spring tension beneath the head of the fastener, whereas flat washers and fender washers, whether metal, nylon or rubber, are simply flat spacers meant to spread out the load by creating a larger area for the point of contact.

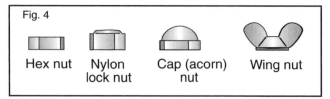

Fig. 4

| Hex nut | Nylon lock nut | Cap (acorn) nut | Wing nut |

Unlike other washers, the finishing washer is often selected more for its appearance than its ability to help spread a load. Finishing washers provide an attractive method of surface mounting fasteners that have a countersunk head.

Nuts used for marine applications are shown in Figure 4. The most frequently used are the nylon lock nut and the cap nut, both of which are made from stainless steel. Nylon lock nuts can be found

RULE of THUMB

Enlarging the area of contact increases the effective holding capacity of the fastener.

almost everywhere on board because they hold more securely than other types due to a nylon insert on the exit end of the nut.

A cap nut — or acorn nut — creates an attractive appearance while holding a fastener secure. Cap nuts are typically seen on the ends of fasteners that extend into the cabin such as those on a headsail track, rope clutch or a deck organizer. A common hex nut is often used in combination with a cap nut for additional security.

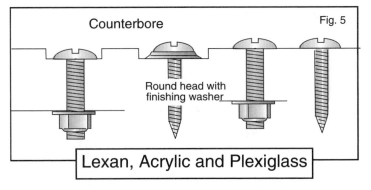

Counterbore   Fig. 5

Round head with finishing washer

Lexan, Acrylic and Plexiglass

Wing nuts are used sparingly on boats, and are found only on items that will likely be removed or serviced on a regular basis. The most common use of wing nuts on a boat are on the posts of batteries and sea strainers, since batteries are replaced every few seasons, and a sea strainer may require weekly service. The need for tools is eliminated if wing nuts are used instead of hex nuts.

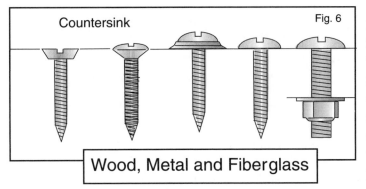

Countersink   Fig. 6

Wood, Metal and Fiberglass

Although it is possible to use most any fastener with almost any material, some combinations are more secure than others. When working with plastics, for instance, a round head or pan head fastener is the best choice, and should be installed on a flush surface or recessed with a counterbore (Fig. 5). A counterbore is made instead of a countersink because of the elastic nature of plastics; a countersunk screw can often be tightened to the point that it pulls completely through the material or cracks the plastic.

For metals and wood, a countersink (Fig. 6) is ideal in combination with a variety of fastener types — sheet metal screws (oval head or flat head), countersunk machine screws (oval head or flat head) or wood screws.

TIP:

A quick fix in wood is to insert a wooden toothpick into the hole and reinsert the fastener. The longevity of this repair is questionable.

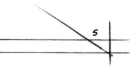

Repairing a hole

If you are drilling new holes, there should be no problem matching the hole to the size of the fastener. But if you are replacing a fastener or if a screw has pulled out of a hole, it would be advisable to repair the hole. Of course, it is possible that a larger fastener would make a hole repair unnecessary, but a larger screw may not fit existing hardware or will look out of proportion with the surrounding area. If the existing hole is in a metal material, little can be done to make a repair. But if the material is fiberglass, wood or plastic, much can be done to preserve its original appearance.

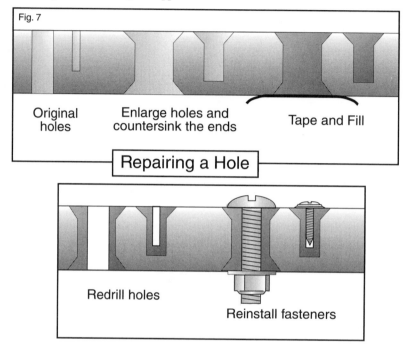

Fig. 7

Original holes   Enlarge holes and countersink the ends   Tape and Fill

Repairing a Hole

Redrill holes

Reinstall fasteners

Begin an effective repair by enlarging the hole to a diameter at least twice the original size (Fig. 7). Using a countersink on a drill or a similar cutting tool, expand the opening of the hole. If the fastener will be through-bolted, expand both sides of opening as shown, and remove the debris. If the hole extends all the way through the material, place a piece of duct tape or masking tape over one end of the hole.

If the hole is in fiberglass, fill the hole with epoxy or a repair product such as Marine-Tex. If the hole is in wood, combine some sawdust with epoxy and fill the hole with this mixture. In either case, completely fill the opening and allow the filler to cure.

Remove any tape and redrill the hole to the correct diameter for the fastener. If the new screw is a machine screw, install it with the appropriate washer and nut. If the application is exposed to the elements, use a good sealant, such as caulk or silicone. Be generous but neat with the sealant, and remove any excess immediately.

This process of filling a hole with epoxy, then redrilling, has a second distinct advantage — moisture cannot affect the surrounding area even after the sealant has deteriorated.

Although it takes a little extra effort to install fasteners correctly, the extra time you spend now will pay you dividends for years in water entry prevention and security of the fitting.

Chapter Two
Holding It All Together

Boat repairs and upgrades are a combination of several elements: the component itself, the adaptation necessary to install it and the final attachment of the item. Without doubt, the possible combinations of these aspects for almost any project can be confusing. Which product to buy, how to best use it, and how to be certain that the installation will be as permanent and attractive as possible are all very real concerns. So how do you know what to do?

When making decisions about products and installation, the old standards are still valid: 1. Ask the advice of knowledgeable friends or salespeople regarding the best product for your budget and application. In general, the product that fits your needs, desires and budget is usually a pretty easy decision to make. 2. Contact a specialist who is familiar with the type of installation you want to do. The best method of installing that product is often fairly obvious, regardless of the complexity involved in making it work. 3. Study the installation recommendations provided by the product's manufacturer. How best to go about actually doing the installation often seems to be the biggest cause of confusion. And with good reason.

There are half a dozen types of masking tape and at least an equal number of sealants. Then there are the adhesives — epoxies, wood glue, polysulfites, polyurethanes and cements, to name a few. The decision can be mind-boggling, but it doesn't have to be. Ask yourself the following questions:

- Is this a permanent installation, or will it need to be removed occasionally?
- Does it need to be sealed against the weather?
- What materials are involved — wood, fiberglass, metal, acrylic, plastic?
- Do the materials involved require separation from one another?

Even after you have answered these questions, other considerations still remain. You will probably need metal fasteners, and you will certainly need tools. A work plan would be good and, of course, you will need time. Lots and lots of time. But don't despair. Breaking down the project into several steps in turn simplifies the process.

Consider what will hold everything together.

Metal fasteners aside, the materials used to hold a project together can be generally divided into three categories: sealants, adhesives and tapes. Although some adhesives are intended to perform the dual function of also sealing two pieces together, there is usually a good reason for using one material instead of another.

Sealants (Fig. 1) are comprised primarily of caulk, silicone and double-sided adhesive strips. Although these materials are intended to stick to the surfaces to which they are applied, they are not intended to hold those surfaces together without the aid of mechanical fasteners.

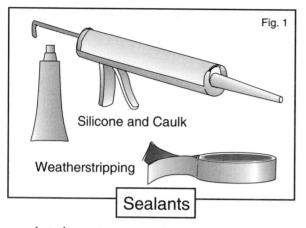

Fig. 1

Silicone and Caulk

Weatherstripping

Sealants

• **Caulk**, a sealant with a limited life span, is customarily used for applications in which a gap is being filled. It is typically used, for example, to fill the gaps between planks of a teak deck. Available in either white or black, caulk is designed to be replaced periodically; it is easy to apply and relatively easy to remove.

• **Silicone** is also designed to fill gaps; however, it has a longer life expectancy than caulk due to its greater degree of elasticity. This means that, in general, silicone will perform its job for a longer period of time than caulk before replacement is required. Silicone is most commonly used in applications that require a weather-proof seal such as deck plates for vents, the trim rings on opening ports, and inspection cover plates.

Silicone is often used to create a watertight gasket. For example, when installing a hand pump on a marine head, it is advisable to apply silicone between the base of the pump and the mounting plate. The fasteners on the pump should not be tightened down completely until the silicone has had a chance to cure. Once cured, the silicone will perform the function of a watertight gasket as the fasteners are snugged down.

Another primary use of silicone is creating a barrier between dissimilar materials in an effort to prevent electrolysis. This is important when installing a stainless steel fitting on an aluminum surface such as a cheek block on a boom for reefing, or a halyard restraint to assist an upper furling swivel. Like caulk, silicone is easy to apply and remove; unlike caulk, silicone can often be found in white, black or clear. Both sealants are supplied in small toothpaste-size tubes as well as large cartridges intended for use with a caulking gun.

RULE OF THUMB

Comparing adhesives and sealants: Many adhesives are also excellent sealants but, unlike sealants, adhesives are not meant to be easily removed. In addition, adhesives are greater in variety because they tend to be more specialized.

- **Adhesive foam strips**. This type of "sealant" is not considered strictly a sealant, but it does perform much the same function. Single or double-sided adhesive strips are primarily used as weatherstripping to reduce noise and the abrasion caused by two surfaces vibrating against each other. These strips are handy for placement under the lids of lazarettes, for example, or the covers on an engine compartment.

Adhesives (Fig. 2) are intended to bond two or more surfaces together, with the permanency of the bond being dependent upon which adhesive is used.

- **Polysulfites** are often used like caulk to fill gaps between two surfaces; however, a polysulfite will create adhesion of one surface to another. Polysulfites come in two varieties — two-part systems that use a chemical catalyst to accelerate curing, and one-part systems that draw moisture from the air. Two-part polysulfites cure more quickly.

Although this type of adhesive forms an excellent permanent bond, it must still be used with mechanical fasteners.

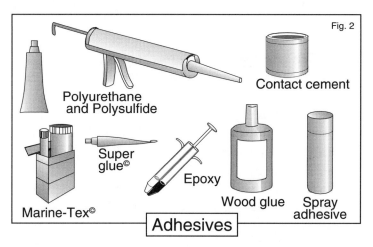

Fig. 2

Polyurethane and Polysulfide

Contact cement

Super glue©

Epoxy

Wood glue

Spray adhesive

Marine-Tex©

Adhesives

CAUTIONS!: 1) Polysulfites will melt plastics and, 2) if used with teak, a primer is necessary otherwise the bond will pull away from the wood's oily surface.

- **Polyurethanes** create a permanent bond. This adhesive should be used only for installations in which removal is not expected to occur. Examples of this type of installation are hull/deck joints, thru-hull fittings, opening ports or hatches. Polyurethanes can be used with virtually any material, and are often found in wood-to-fiberglass projects.

RULE of THUMB:

Many small projects can be completed using a polyurethane adhesive only, eliminating the need for mechanical fasteners.

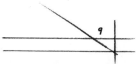

Before working with a polyurethane adhesive, *several cautions are worth considering:*

1. **Polyurethane creates a permanent bond**. This means that it will be permanently attached to your clothing as well as any other surface it touches. Be certain any excess is wiped away immediately with kerosene or mineral spirits.

2. **Most polyurethanes require several hours, or even several days, to cure**. If this adhesive is used outdoors, it would be wise to protect the area from the elements until curing has been completed.

3. **If you use polyurethane on fiberglass, expect gelcoat damage when this adhesive is removed**. Polyurethanes tend to "burn" the surfaces they touch as part of the bonding process.

4. **Polyurethanes are not designed for use on teak decks**. Many teak cleaners will soften the adhesion of the bond.

Comparing polysulfites and polyurethanes

These adhesives have two features in common: They are supplied in either small tubes or large cartridges, and they offer many of the same benefits as a sealant, i.e. flexibility to the bond.

Other adhesives used for more specialized purposes

Other bonding materials, shown in Figure 2, are adhesives only. They offer none of the flexibility of a sealant.

- **Contact cement** is commonly used for projects that require strong adhesion between two surfaces, but where no stress is applied, such as the installation of soundproofing in an engine compartment. Both materials, in this case fiberglass or wood and foam insulation, are given a coat of cement. After the cement has been allowed to dry for 20-30 minutes, the two surfaces are pressed together.

- **Spray adhesive**, used only for light applications, provides a temporary bond between two surfaces. For example, spray adhesive might be used to glue two pieces of paper together or to attach a clear cover sheet to a chart or document for protection. Like contact cement, spray adhesive works best when both surfaces to be joined are coated with the adhesive.

- **Wood glue**, available in hardware stores, works well to form a nearly permanent bond between two pieces of non-oily wood (oak, maple, ash, etc). Both surfaces are coated and then pressed together while still wet. Wood glue works best when mechanical fasteners or clamps are used until the bond has cured. Often, two pieces of wood bonded with a wood glue cannot be separated without significant damage even if no fasteners have been used.

- **Epoxy** can also be used to join two pieces of wood. In fact, epoxy can be used to join just about anything to just about anything else. Epoxy offers no

TIP:

When using contact cement, be certain that everything has been positioned correctly; repositioning is difficult.

flexibility, and therefore should not be used with materials that are not rigid (such as sound insulation) or for installations in which the materials tend to flex during use. For example, epoxy would be an excellent choice to repair the wood and fiberglass lid of a propane locker, but would be a poor choice for the locker itself, due to the likelihood of flexing while underway.

Epoxies are a two-part adhesive; until they are mixed, no bond is possible. The components must be used in equal amounts; otherwise the bond will cure too fast or, in extreme cases, not at all. Epoxy generally requires several hours to set; however, once cured, the bond cannot be separated without damage to the surface of the materials.

- **Super Glue** is the best-known trade name for a thin, fast-curing adhesive that has uncountable uses in light duty applications. Minor repairs such as a split instrument cover, or a broken ceramic or plastic knob are the forte of this adhesive. When originally introduced, this adhesive performed its job so well that people were gluing their fingers together. Today, it is no longer quite that strong, but is still effective enough to securely repair most small projects. This adhesive is most effective when used in conjunction with fasteners.

- **Marine-Tex** is a white or grey hybrid adhesive that is applied like a two-part epoxy and requires about the same curing time, but has much of the flexibility of a polysulfite or polyurethane. Used primarily for small repairs, this adhesive can often be found where temperature extremes might cause a different adhesive to fail. Examples of Marine-Tex use are repairs to the interior of an icebox or the mixing elbow of an engine exhaust, as well as a myriad of miscellaneous small problems belowdecks. *Note: When exposed to the sun for long periods, Marine-Tex will turn yellow. For this reason, it is not a good substitute for white gelcoat on exterior fiberglass.*

Tapes

When it comes to tapes, shown in Figure 3, each one has a specific task for which it was designed. Although there is some overlap of purpose, in reality you will likely end up with several different types in your toolbag or dockbox. In addition to the types of tape listed below, there are other specialty tapes on the market. However, few others relate to marine applications to the same degree as those mentioned here.

- **Weather-resistant tape** — generally referred to as Long Mask masking tape, 3M's version of this product — is primarily used to protect gelcoat or painted areas adjacent to wood while the wood is being refinished. Long mask is available in several types, each of which is designated with a different color:
  - **Tan** must be removed within 24 hours to avoid leaving adhesive behind.
  - **Green** can remain in place for three to five days, depending upon the temperature, without leaving a gooey residue behind.
  - **Blue** can remain for up to seven days without a clean-up problem.

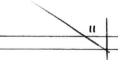

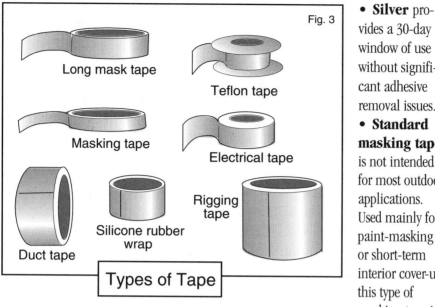

Types of Tape

Fig. 3

Long mask tape

Teflon tape

Masking tape

Electrical tape

Duct tape

Silicone rubber wrap

Rigging tape

- **Silver** provides a 30-day window of use without significant adhesive removal issues.
- **Standard masking tape** is not intended for most outdoor applications. Used mainly for paint-masking or short-term interior cover-up, this type of masking tape is cheap, tears easily and comes off clean even if left in place for extended periods of time indoors.

Both standard tape and Long-Mask masking tape are available in a variety of sizes up to 2" wide.

- **Duct tape** (not duck tape!) is the long-standing general-purpose favorite for almost any application of mending, sealing or binding. Originally developed to seal air conditioner ducts to plenums, duct tape holds well even when wet, rendering it ideal for temporary repairs such as a split water hose. Although duct tape lends itself to countless applications, it leaves behind a messy residue that can only be removed with solvents.

- **Silicone rubber wrap** is nearly as versatile as duct tape. Sticking only to itself and designed to create waterproof electrical connections, silicone rubber wrap can also be used to create non-slip grips on tools, to whip the ends of rope or to make an emergency repair to exhaust or water lines. This type of tape has a great deal of elasticity and will stretch up to three times its normal length, producing a surface tension that helps to keep it in place. This material is impervious to oil, diesel fuel, salt water and extremes of temperature, making it a good choice for temporary engine-related repairs.

- **Teflon tape** is convenient for sealing water pipes and hoses without messy sealants: Simply wrap it around the male threaded end of a fitting before making the final hose connection.

RULE of THUMB

Heat shrink tubing, like a silicone rubber wrap, will seal electrical connections and keep them dry even in a wet area. Unlike a silicone wrap, however, heat shrink is not to be used for hose and tubing repair.

In addition, Teflon tape is often used on the threads of stainless steel machine screws when attaching gear to an aluminum surface; this helps prevent electrolysis between the dissimilar metals.

- **Electrical tape** is perhaps the most familiar of all. Unlike silicone rubber wrap, electrical tape contains an adhesive that will allow it to stick to surfaces other than itself. Unlike silicone wrap, electrical tape is not intended for wet applications. Best suited for wrapping wire connections in a dry area, electrical tape is available in a fairly wide range of colors, allowing the color of the tape to match the color of the wire insulation. In a multiple contractor environment, different colors of tape can be used to help isolate and distinguish which worker completed which phase of the work.

- **Rigging tape**, similar to silicone rubber wrap, will stick only to itself. Rigging tape is meant for covering the sharp points on split rings and cotter pins used to install standing rigging. Rigging tape has a great deal of elasticity and will stretch up to three times its length, producing a surface tension similar to a rubber wrap.

Chapter Three
Tools of the Trade

In one way or another, most of us have made compromises in our boats relative to size, functionality or aesthetics. A bigger boat can solve inconveniences found on a smaller boat. You may decide to minimize performance in order to maximize accommodations and comfort. The one constant, regardless of boat size, is the need for more storage space: Almost all of us continually search for ways to stow more and more of our possessions on board.

Most skippers I know arrange the cabin so that gear is both easy to reach and secure. But they typically don't give the lazarettes in the cockpit a second thought. Why not? When you think of it, lazarettes are a much-forgotten, yet invaluable, source of storage space and particularly handy for tools.

Whether you spend days, weekends or long holidays on your boat, or even live aboard, your tools and access to them are a necessity. With storage space at a premium, accessibility is a challenge to say the least; a well-organized lazarette will save you untold aggravation. If you start now creating a toolbag that has the greatest range of use and requires minimal storage space, you will reap the rewards in saved time and aggravation. Let's take a look at what comprises a complete, yet compact, toolbag.

The right collection of tools will help you perform three basic types of repairs, from mechanical to electrical to plumbing tasks. Mechanical repairs might include removing and rebedding stanchions or installing a new block. Electrical repairs can range from rewiring a cabin light to rewiring the entire boat. As for plumbing repairs, a typical project might include replacing fresh water lines or installing a head repair kit on a commode.

As you might suspect, most projects will include elements of two or more of these repair categories. This is why it is essential that your toolbag be as diverse as possible — without wasting money or storage space for rarely needed tools. Let's start with tool basics, which includes most mechanical repairs and, along the way, review how these hand tools are best used.

Screwdrivers are the most used of any tool in your bag. You need two types: Phillips and slotted or, as my son calls them, plus and minus (what they look like when viewed from the working end of the blade). The Phillips screwdrivers will be used the most, so be certain these tools are of the highest quality.

Ideally, your inventory would include at least two tip sizes for each type — Phillips sizes #1 and #2, and slotted tip sizes of ¼" and ³⁄₁₆" — as well as at least two shank lengths each. These are shown in Figure 1. For difficult-to-reach places and those with little clearance, it is often helpful to own a "stubby" version of each screwdriver type.

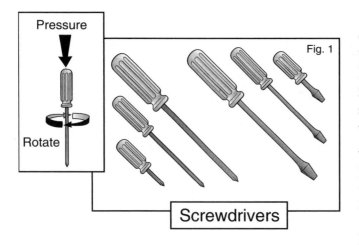

Using a screwdriver. Remember that you are more likely to damage the fastener head with a screwdriver than with any other tool. And, once the damage is done it is nearly impossible to remove the fastener. (I've been there; haven't you?) A screwdriver will cause the least amount of damage if forceful downward pressure is applied on the top of the handle while the tool is rotated (Fig. 1 inset). If the fastener refuses to move, this method will generally result in the least amount of damage to the head.

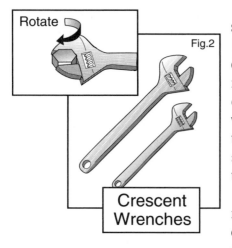

Crescent wrenches (Fig. 2) are the second most frequently used tool. One small (6") and one medium (8") wrench will handle just about any bolt head or nut that you might encounter. With a thumb wheel used to quickly adjust the opening of the jaw, these wrenches grip a standard six-sided nut on two to four of its sides. For extra leverage, slip a short length of pipe over the end of the wrench.

Whether you use an extension handle or not, be certain to attach the tool so that you can apply pressure with the fixed side of the jaw facing the direction of rotation (Fig. 2 inset). Often the wrench works well even if you apply pressure with the jaws in the wrong position; but if the fastener resists, you may only succeed in rounding off its corners. When a more secure grip is required, consider using a combination wrench.

Open end/combination wrenches (Fig. 3) are open at one end, with a shape similar to the jaws of an adjustable wrench. The opposite end, intended to fit a six- or eight-sided bolt or nut, is enclosed. Most skippers purchase a set of wrenches to fit six-sided fasteners — the most common shape.

RULE of THUMB

Though it is less expensive (and more compact) to purchase a screwdriver handle that has interchangeable tips, rarely are the tips made of high quality metals. The result is that the tips are more likely to break and the metal parts are more subject to rust. Consider planning for the longer term.

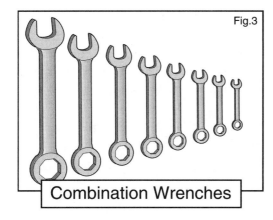

Combination Wrenches

Although combination wrenches can be acquired individually, they are usually purchased in sets of eight; both metric and SAE versions are available. Investigate which type of fasteners are most prevalent on your boat, then buy that version of wrenches. To cover the greatest scope of potential use, choose two sizes of adjustable wrenches and a set of combination wrenches.

A **socket set** (Fig. 4), if good quality, will last for years and still look great. Be certain that the handle has a locking mechanism to prevent the socket from coming off accidentally. (On land, the socket would simply fall to the ground but, on a boat, it is likely to disappear overboard.)

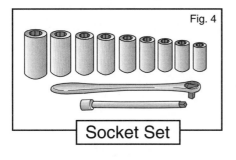

Socket Set

When you buy sockets, I would strongly suggest that you purchase the long barrel type. Shanks on many machine screws used on boats extend well beyond the washer and nut; without a deep barrel, a socket might be unusable. As with the combination wrenches, you will need to decide whether SAE or metric would be more useful.

There are several variables to consider when choosing a set of sockets. In addition to whether a socket is metric or SAE, a socket may be six-, eight- or twelve-sided; decide which version is best suited to the fasteners on your boat. In my experience, most mid-priced production boats call for six-sided sockets.

Locking pliers (Fig. 5) are another useful type of bolt and nut grabber. Often called a Visegrip — the best-known brand of locking pliers — these tools are sometimes the only ones that will budge a stubborn bolt. Like adjustable open-end wrenches, an assortment of one small and one medium sized tool is recommended, along with a third that is usually a smaller pliers with tapered jaws.

Locking pliers can be clamped down so tightly on a corroded bolt or rusted nut

TIP:

You will likely acquire both SAE and metric sockets eventually. But at the outset, in the interest of conserving space and expense, choose one or the other.

The fixed side of locking pliers is the handle with the thumbscrew.

that either the item in question will rotate or the bolt will shear off. Rarely will the nut or bolt remain in place unchanged. Locking pliers are attached to the head of a fastener in the same orientation as an adjustable wrench (Fig. 5 inset), with the "fixed" side of the jaws toward the direction of rotation. For extra leverage, a short length of pipe can be slipped over the fixed handle in a fashion similar to an adjustable wrench.

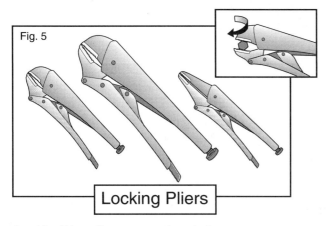

Fig. 5

Locking Pliers

Non-locking pliers complete the list of general purpose gripping tools. Two types are generally needed — a standard adjustable pliers and a long-nose version (Fig. 6). Although some repair contractors prefer to substitute slip-jaw pliers for the standard type, two pieces should still be sufficient. Even though there is no real "fixed" side to most types of pliers, it is good practice to orient the lower of the two jaws toward the direction of rotation when possible (Fig. 6, inset A).

Slip-jaw pliers are the exception to this general rule. Here, like locking pliers, there is a very definite fixed side. The fixed jaw is the side with the "S" shape to the upper portion of the handle (Fig. 6, inset B).

Specialty wrenches are used only occasionally on boats, but no doubt you will eventually accumulate them all.

A **spanner wrench** is used to remove the top from many brands of sea strainers, including those made by Perko and Groco. This tool has one rigid arm and one arm on a pivot. By adjusting the position of the movable arm, a spanner wrench can be used on a wide variety of caps (Fig. 7, inset A).

Packing nut wrenches, as the name implies, are used to tighten the packing nuts on the prop shaft. Used in pairs, these

TIP:

If you can afford it, a high-power (12 volt or greater) rechargeable drill is the optimum choice.

RULE of THUMB

I highly recommend using hole saw sizes above 3" only in combination with a 1/2" or larger drill, due to the substantial amount of torque needed to cut such large diameter openings. Although a smaller drill might do the job, the possibility exists that such use would permanently damage the drill. If you must cut large openings (4" to 5"), such as those required for the installation of deck vents, it is often best to rent a 1/2" drill from a tool supply house.

wrenches apply pressure in opposite directions in order to secure the seal on the packing gland (Fig. 7, inset B).

Hex key wrenches find uses aboard a boat in such places as the setscrews on bimini frames or in fasteners for the faceplates used on some barometers and clocks. Additional reasons to own a set of hex key wrenches include the collar for a drill bit, the blade on a jigsaw and the centering of a mandrel. Typically, these wrenches come in sets that fold into a handle; this compactness combined with modest cost allows you to own both a metric and SAE version.

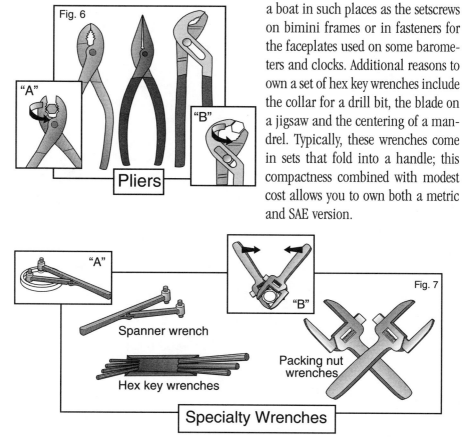

Fig. 6

"A"

"B"

Pliers

"A"

"B"

Fig. 7

Spanner wrench

Hex key wrenches

Packing nut wrenches

Specialty Wrenches

Must-have power tools

An electric drill (Fig. 8) is the most important power tool you can own. There are many choices to consider, but when selecting a drill for general-purpose use, nothing beats a corded ¼" variable speed reversible drill with a keyless chuck.

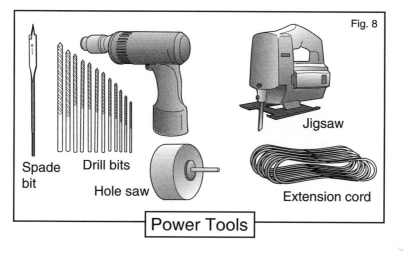

Fig. 8

Spade bit

Drill bits

Hole saw

Jigsaw

Extension cord

Power Tools

Accessories. You will need a set of drill bits, in at least eight sizes from $\frac{1}{16}$" to $\frac{1}{4}$", with tips made from tungsten, carbide or diamond dust. Although drilling into aluminum is no big deal, if you expect to drill stainless steel you must have this type of drill bit. I also recommend a $\frac{1}{2}$" spade bit. The holes made by a spade bit provide a way to insert the blade of a jigsaw into a fiberglass, metal or wood surface when making a cutout. Other useful drill attachments are a countersink and screwdriver bits.

A set of **hole saws**, supplied in kit form with a mandrel and several interchangeable sizes, can make short work of many tasks. Cutting through a stringer in order to run plumbing lines, cutting through a hatch when installing a solar deck vent, or cutting a passageway through a bulkhead for stereo speaker wire or electrical cables are all prime uses of hole saws.

A **jigsaw** is the easiest way to cut an opening for the installation of anything from a radio to locker doors. If you would like to standardize on one type of blade, purchase "bi- metal" blades with at least 24 teeth to the inch (32 is even better). This type of blade can be used with fiberglass, metal or wood, and will always leave a fine, clean edge. Use lower speeds with fiberglass and wood, and higher speeds with metals; go along slowly as you follow your marks.

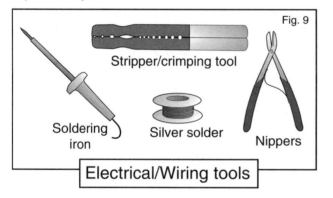

Fig. 9

Stripper/crimping tool

Soldering iron   Silver solder   Nippers

Electrical/Wiring tools

An **extension cord**, unquestionably needed, should be insulated in a round casing (less prone to tangle), made with at least 14 gauge wire (12 gauge would be even better), and fitted with a three-prong grounded plug.

Specialty tools

A **crimping tool** (Fig. 9) is essential when dealing with electricity and wiring. This multi-purpose tool can strip up to eight sizes of wire as well as crimp three sizes of butt connectors, ring terminals and spade terminals. Unfortunately, when cutting wire, a crimping tool leaves something to be desired.

Wire nippers — or "dikes" as they are sometimes called — cut wire cleanly. Nippers can be used to strip the insulation from wire, but will usually take off a few strands of wire along with the insulation. The two tools together, however, provide the best means of handling almost any size of wire and just about any wire connector.

A **soldering iron** or soldering gun is used to permanently fasten two or more wires together. For delicate work, which includes

RULE of THUMB

When tapping a hole, always use a lubricant such as WD-40 to help dissipate the heat produced when the tap cuts into metal.

most applications aboard a boat, an iron is preferable to a gun. (A soldering gun is typically too hot for most uses, and will tend to melt the insulation as well as burn the surrounding surface.) A soldering iron works well with its lower heat, is smaller and lighter, and has a long tapered tip that helps get into small spaces. With either type, silver solder is the best choice for secure, long-lasting connections. *Note: Although butt connectors will successfully join together two or more wires, I prefer the security of wires that have been bonded together with solder.*

Miscellaneous tools, shown in Figure 10, are occasional use tools for which there are no good substitutes. A small (6") **level** is indispensable when matching the lines of an existing shelf, or installing a new one, by using the bubble indicators.

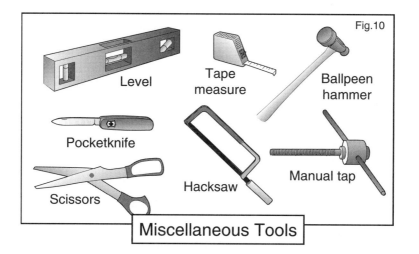

Fig.10

Level — Tape measure — Ballpeen hammer

Pocketknife

Scissors — Hacksaw — Manual tap

Miscellaneous Tools

A **tape measure** of at least 10' in length is ideal for most projects; a fabric tape will outlast one made with a metal rule. A **ballpeen hammer** is useful for coercing a stubborn rudder post collar or checking the deck for areas of delamination.

A **manual tap** is useful over and over again when installing blocks, tracks and other gear in fiberglass and metal. Be certain to buy the correct size drill bits for the machine screws you use the most, usually #8 and #10.

A **hacksaw** can make quick work of shortening bolts, cutting plastic and metal tubing, or trimming heavy metal sheets for such items as backing plates. Use fine-toothed blades (24 to 32 teeth per inch) for a clean edge and minimal filing.

Throw **scissors** and a **pocketknife** into your toolbag for hundreds of little jobs. My choice for a pocketknife is a Swiss Army knife model "Explorer"; it seems to always have just the right blade or accessory, including a corkscrew for the end of the day.

Optional power tools

The power tools shown in Figure 11 may or may not be needed on your boat. If you hire out the thankless job of polishing your boat, you will have little need for an **electric buffer**. If, however, you decide to take on the task of polishing smooth fiberglass surfaces yourself, the typical buffer used for the purpose is fitted with 8" accessories, has two speeds and is made in a corded version only.

CAUTION: It is CRITICAL that you be acutely aware of the electric cord attached to the handle as well as any nearby lines. If the buffer becomes fouled, it can quite literally jump out of your hands. The potential danger of this activity cannot be overstated.

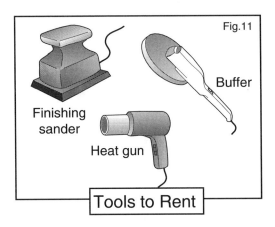

Tools to Rent

Fig.11

Finishing sander

Buffer

Heat gun

If your vessel is blessed with generous amounts of exterior teak, which you maintain yourself, you will need a **heat gun**, **scraping tools** and an **electric sander**. A good heat gun can be found at most hardware stores, and will have two power settings, (the higher at about 2200 watts). If accessory tips are offered, decline them.

Scraping tools used for teak refinishing are not as coarse as those sold for removing house paint. Ask a marine supplier for small, long-handled scraping tools with a variety of interchangeable blade shapes.

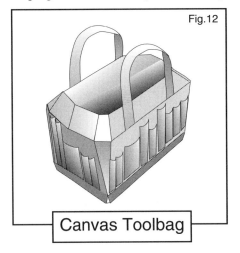

Canvas Toolbag

Fig.12

An electric sander useful for preparing teak can be either a 4" finishing sander or a 5" orbital sander. The finishing sander is less expensive, but the orbital sander handles heavier work should the need arise. Since a sander is used only two or three times a year to refinish teak, an inexpensive unit will last a long time and do a fine job if you take your time.

Your toolbag

Now that you have the perfect collection of tools, you will need something to put them in, and nothing works better on board than a tool carrier made from canvas. A good canvas toolbag (Fig. 12) will have several specific features: • heavy canvas fabric • reinforced handles and underside • dozens of vertical exterior pockets • an easily accessed interior • no feet of any kind

When the toolbag is full it might require a block and tackle to lift it, but at least all of your tools will be organized in a compact, easy-to-access carrier.

Well, there you have my recommendations. You may acquire other tools over time, but if your toolbag includes those presented here it is unlikely that you will come up short in the middle of a project.

Chapter Four
Control Lines to the Cockpit

Leading lines aft to the cockpit is pretty much standard practice these days, but this upgrade remains one of the most popular changes made to an older boat. As it turns out, it is also one of the easiest to accomplish. Like almost any other "home" project, three constants apply: • always measure twice and cut once • the project will require fourfold the amount of time that you estimate • it will likely cost twice as much as you might guess.

The reconfiguration shown here involved four blocks at the base of the mast leading to two double rope deck organizers, which in turn led to two double rope clutches and a cam cleat near the cockpit on each side of the companionway. The mainsheet had already been led aft to a port winch on the cabin top, leaving the main halyard, the topping lift, and two reef lines to be brought back. Ultimately, the main halyard and first reef were to be led to a rope clutch on the starboard side, while the mainsheet and second reef would lead to a rope clutch to port. The topping lift was destined to terminate at a clam cleat on the port side.

Many sailboats have keel-stepped masts, including the O'Day 28 that was the focus of this upgrade. When a keel-stepped mast is present, there is almost always a plate on the cabin top that surrounds the mast (Fig. 1). This plate is often configured with as many as six slots that allow the insertion of thick "U" shaped brackets, which in turn are meant to provide attachment points for as many as six blocks — two to port, two to starboard, and two directly aft of the mast. Unfortunately, not every mast is stepped properly and, when this happens, the "U" brackets are usually omitted. A modification of this type becomes more expensive and involved than it should be when minor hardware is not put into place as originally intended.

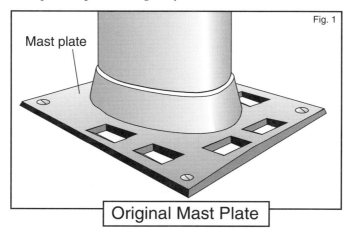

Fig. 1

Mast plate

Original Mast Plate

This mast plate was sealed in place with 3M 5200, or a similar material. The result was that any attempt to remove the plate would likely cause damage to the cabin top, or at the very least result in the need for cosmetic repair. In addition, there was a ½" pin running horizontally through the mast and resting on the collar. In short, untensioning the standing rigging, unstepping the mast with a rented crane, and somehow removing the mast plate were far more complicated and costly than I wanted. A simpler alternative was called for. If the mast had been unstepped and the plate removed, a cleaner cabin top would have been created, but using the mast plate did not appear to be a cost-effective option. Instead, I decided to install separate blocks on deck at the base of the mast.

Since Schaefer Marine was the supplier of the blocks on board — and I'm the type of person that likes the look of matched original equipment — I chose the same make for all additional blocks. I investigated "halyard" blocks, but I was not satisfied with the lead from the base of the mast. I selected spring-loaded stand-up swivel blocks due to the wider variety of placement options and lead-in angles they provided. The stand-up blocks would turn the main halyard and first reef to starboard, while the topping lift and second reef went to port. The running rigging is ⅜" which called for four of Schaefer's part number #05-62. These swivel blocks were complete with plastic mounting plates, and were tall enough to keep the lines off the deck to avoid potential chafing across the non-skid. (Larger boats don't have as steeply curved a cabin top, but for many smaller sailboats this can be a problem.)

Like so many other production boats both then and now, the cabin roof is constructed of approximately ¼" fiberglass, ½" balsa core, and another ¼" of fiberglass (Fig. 2 inset). Please note the word "approximately"; typically, the deck is not the same thickness fore to aft alongside the mast, so be aware that different lengths of fasteners may be necessary if you want to create a clean finish inside the cabin. In this instance, the blocks that were mounted near the rear of the mast for the reefing lines required 1½" #10 bolts, but the forward blocks needed only 1¼".

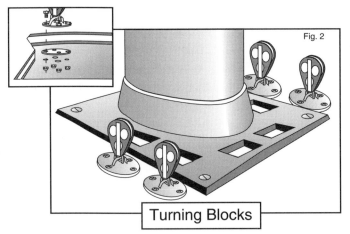

Fig. 2

Turning Blocks

The blocks were originally bolted down (Fig. 2) using fender washers along with nylon locking nuts on the inside of the cabin, but I was satisfied with neither the appearance nor the imagined strength of the installation. After all, the main halyard and the first reef line have to withstand a substantial amount of stress. The fender washers were soon replaced with stainless steel backing plates that had been special ordered direct from Schaefer. The backing plates were the same stainless disks used for the base of the #05-62 standup swivel blocks, without the eyebolt for a becket. This installation has permitted continued trouble-free operation.

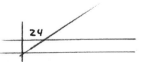

Be certain to use a sealant under the nylon mount plates to keep moisture where it belongs — out. For this installation, I used 3M 5200 beneath the blocks as well as *inside* the drilled hole in order to provide extra protection for the balsa core. All blocks were mounted as close as possible to the mast plate and, for a neat appearance, the holes for the bolts were lined up in a "diamond" shape when viewed from fore to aft.

The next part involves turning the lines aft from the blocks at the base of the mast (Fig. 3). For this, I used two-rope deck organizers (Schaefer part #05-80), one on each side of the cabin top. These were supplied with ¼-20 machine screws that were 3½" long which had to be replaced with fasteners that were 2½" long — 1" for the depth of the block and 1" through the cabin top. Unfortunately, I was unable to find backing plates for these organizers so, instead, fender washers and nylon locking nuts were used along with sealant. This has held up well, but I would recommend checking the tightness of the screws at the beginning of each season.

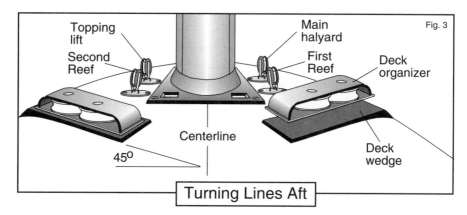

Topping lift

Second Reef

Main halyard

First Reef

Deck organizer

Fig. 3

Centerline

45⁰

Deck wedge

Turning Lines Aft

The angle at which the deck organizers are set is something close to 45 degrees off the centerline of the boat, but the issue to be aware of is deck curvature. In the location at which the organizers were used, the cabin top curve is sufficient to create the need for a shim between the block and the deck. Although these organizers are very well made, to insure the smoothest operation in these instances, I recommend the use of a shim to avoid the possibility of binding the sheaves. I used a shaped piece of teak that was ½" on one end, tapered to a sharp edge, and was the dimension of the organizer; a Dremel tool made quick work of shaping the wood.

Drill a hole for the inboard bolt first; tighten it down by hand, then mark and drill the hole for the outboard fastener. In this manner, you will maintain the straightest possible line through the block into the deck as well as testing whether or not the shim is of the proper thickness. When drilling the hole, tape the shim in place under the block to ensure proper positioning.

The final location of the turning blocks depends on two dimensions — the width of the sliding companionway hatch and the width of the available space on each side of the companionway through which lines can be led. In any case, the primary goal is a clean lead from the swivel blocks, through the deck organizers and finally alongside the companionway. Careful attention to angles now will result in smoother operation later.

Generally, you have two options for the location of lines alongside the companionway — close alongside the hatch guides or straight through the bases supporting the traveler. On this boat, the traveler is mounted on the cabin atop solid bases of fiberglass and wood, with a narrow space between these bases and the companionway. Two options presented themselves:

1. drill through the traveler bases while holding your breath and trying to miss the three long vertical bolts holding down the traveler track. PVC sleeves could then be inserted in the holes for a finished look, or
2. lead the lines through the narrow space on each side of the companionway and add fairleads below the traveler.

With me, simpler wins almost every time! Of course, if the traveler bases on your boat are open, your decision is obvious.

When making this decision, keep in mind that the farther away from the mast you position the deck organizers, the more curvature you have to deal with; you may still choose this option for a cleaner lead aft. Also remember that as the deck increases in curvature, the shims will increase in depth.

To achieve a final position check for the deck organizers before drilling holes, run a line from a swivel block near the mast, pass it through one of the sheaves of the organizer, run it aft to the cockpit and then tie it off to maintain tension. Take your time to be certain of the position of the deck organizers by moving them around the general area of final installation: After all, you will likely be using this arrangement a long time! Once you are satisfied, drill the holes, apply a sealant to the bottom of the organizer as well as the inside of the holes, and mount the double blocks.

The other major pieces of hardware to install are the rope clutches (Fig. 4). My choice for this was Spinlock XA. (Schaefer would have been nice but they exceeded the budget for this project.) The rope clutches are each held in place with four ¼-20 countersunk bolts that were 1¼" long; of course, fender washers and lock nuts were

RULE of THUMB

This project has held up well, but it has proved to be prudent to check tightness on the screws at the beginning of each season.

Three constants of most "home" projects

1) always measure twice and cut once

2) the project will require fourfold the amount of time it would appear

3) it will likely cost twice as much as you might guess.

also used. If you choose, as I did, to run the lines close beside the rails in which the companionway hatch slides, you will find that the space between the guides and the traveler bases leaves precious little room for positioning the lines. The rope clutches must be mounted as near as possible to the companionway slides, but be aware of the angle of entry that the lines will make into the clutch. Close attention to this entry will mean smoother operation and less chafe. Ideally, the clutches would be just far enough away from the companionway slides to allow for the insertion of a varnish brush.

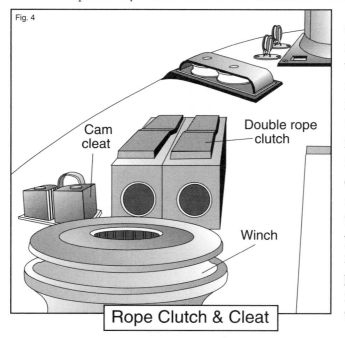

Fig. 4

Cam cleat

Double rope clutch

Winch

Rope Clutch & Cleat

It is quite common on a smaller boat to find that the bases on which the traveler is mounted do not allow for a straight fairlead to the clutch; therefore, a slight angle inward will often produce as clean a lead as possible through the rope clutch. If your traveler is mounted in the cockpit, or your boat is larger, this is not typically an issue.

Turning our attention to the position of the rope clutches relative to the cockpit bulkhead, there is often a mainsheet winch mounted on the cabin top next to the companionway hatch; in fact, sometimes there are two — one on each side of the cabin top. Rope clutches are always mounted forward of these winches, allowing the winches to be used with more than one line. On this boat, there was only a port winch. In an effort to save some money, I removed the halyard winch from the starboard side of the mast, and moved it back to the cabin top to starboard. Although this is not a self-tailing winch like the others on board, the rope clutch is an effective cleat and the winch serves the same purpose on deck as it did on the mast. Later, I bought another winch and mounted it on the mast where the first one had been, making it easier to winch crew up the mast for repairs.

Reeve the lines through the blocks at the base of the mast, through the deck organizers and then to the rope clutches (Fig. 5), lining up the lead as fair as possible while still maintaining tension on the lines. Remove the lines from the clutches, and mark the holes. There will likely be a slight amount of deck curvature at this point, but not enough to cause concern. Once again, check the position of the clutches, verify that the hole marks for the clutches are correct, and then drill.

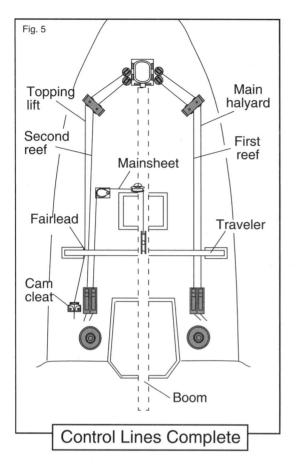

Fig. 5

Topping lift

Main halyard

Second reef

First reef

Mainsheet

Fairlead

Traveler

Cam cleat

Boom

Control Lines Complete

Interior finish of the O'Day 28. Some boats have a solid fiberglass overhead on the ceiling of the cabin interior; some use a soft vinyl liner, and still others employ sections of laminate. In the case of the O'Day 28, the overhead is a fiberglass liner with the composition of the deck above being made up of resin-balsa-resin totaling one inch of thickness. From about the middle of the cabin aft, the interior liner curves away from the core, which results in an air space between the balsa core and the fiberglass on the underside. Fasteners passing through the deck are not seen in the cabin because they stop in this air space at the underside of the deck core, together with washers and nuts. A ¾" hole saw creates access to this air space from inside, while the final trim is provided by dome caps (Fig. 6) that are snapped in place to produce an attractive finish to the ceiling.

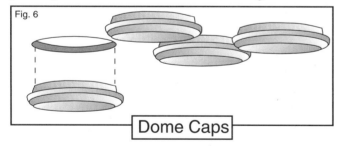

Fig. 6

Dome Caps

This finishing technique was used when the main halyard winch was moved from the mast to the starboard cabin top, and again when the rope clutches were installed. If you use this method, the bolts will be ½" shorter than if they passed through the overhead, and you will need a ¾" hole saw and mandrel to make the cutouts. The dome caps were available from a specialist in O'Day and Cal original parts, D&R Enterprises in East Freeport, MA. I can only assume that similar trims are available for other boats.

After drilling the holes, once again use sealant on the underside of the clutches and the inside of the holes through the deck, then attach the rope clutches to the deck. Except for a cam cleat, all of the cabin top hardware has now been installed for leading the

control lines aft to the cockpit, with a full description of the reefing system installation to follow. *Note: On occasion, upgrades of this type will require additional fairleads between the deck organizers and the rope clutches, but that is the exception and not the rule.*

The topping lift was brought through the port deck organizer along with the second reef, but instead of being led to a rope clutch, the topping lift was terminated at a cam cleat. The reason? The topping lift is typically used in one of two fixed positions — either supporting the boom or releasing it — when raising the mainsail, lowering the mainsail or reefing. The stress on the topping lift is substantially less than the stress on the other lines, so I chose a simpler and less costly option. The cam cleat was mounted next to the port rope clutch on the outboard side, through-bolted in the same manner as the clutches, and was finished with the same dome caps on the interior.

The final activities involve replacing the main halyard, reef lines, and the topping lift with longer lines. The replacement lines were color-coded: blue for the main halyard, red for both of the reef lines, and green for the topping lift. As it happens, the topping lift was long enough to be led back, but was probably in need of replacement anyway due to age. The exact length of replacement lines will be different on each sailboat but, in general, expect to purchase lines that are approximately one and a half times the length of the originals. In addition, allow ten percent more than the measured length for eye splices or knots.

The reefing lines were to be rigged through cheek blocks on both sides of the boom for a single-line, double-reef point system. To me, this represents a major aspect of the aft-led line system because, if it is not done, you must still go to the mast at a time when it would be ideal to remain safely in the cockpit. In other words, without reefing lines also led aft, all of the control is not in the cockpit.

Because I am not an engineer I sometimes overbuild, which is why ⅜" lines were also used for the reefing system. Two cheek blocks from Schaefer (part number 30-09) and one stainless eye strap were mounted on each side of the boom to produce a fixed position slab reefing system at moderate cost. The secret here is to remember to mount the cheek blocks aft of the clews and directly below the cringle to achieve as tight a foot as possible when the system is used.

The first reef point was installed with blocks on the starboard side of the boom (Fig. 7), while the second reef point was installed on the port side of the boom (Fig. 8). This arrangement works and looks best if you can run the lines through the boom; however, even without internal runs the system still provides total control from the cockpit.

The reefing lines are reeved as follows, beginning at the cockpit: forward through the rope clutch to the deck organizer, then to the swivel block at the base of the mast, up to the boom and through the forward sheave, then through to its aft end. From there, up to the first reef clew (port side entry) and down to the aft starboard-mounted cheek block, through the eye strap and on to the forward cheek. The line then is led up to and through the reef cringle that is attached to the starboard side of the main (or through a

29

large grommet), and then finally down to the upper starboard mast cleat and tied off. The same routing would be followed for the second reef but on the port side of the boom.

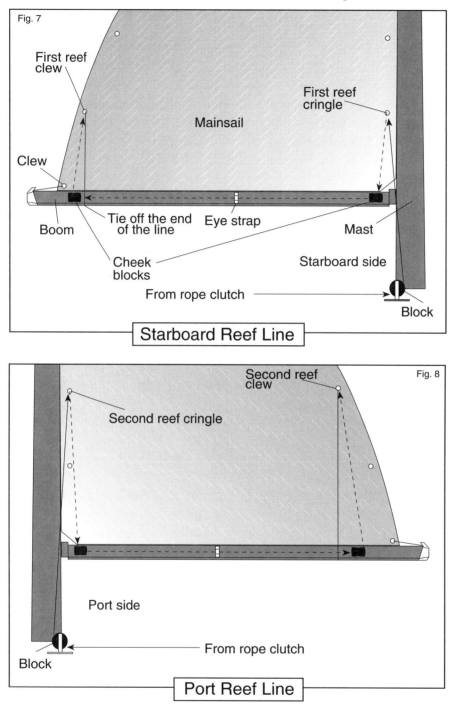

Fig. 7

First reef clew

First reef cringle

Mainsail

Clew

Tie off the end of the line

Eye strap

Boom

Mast

Cheek blocks

Starboard side

From rope clutch

Block

Starboard Reef Line

Second reef clew

Fig. 8

Second reef cringle

Port side

From rope clutch

Block

Port Reef Line

If you work at my pace, this project will require three weekends of half-days of work; I tend to "work" in the morning, and then play in the afternoon.

One last caution: when reeving new lines, take an extra moment to be certain the old and new are firmly attached to each other before using the old line as a messenger. In order to run the reef lines through the boom, as well as run the halyard through the mast, I cut the end of the existing lines as square as possible, wrapped the ends with a small length of masking tape and then butt-stitched the old and new together. This entire connection was also wrapped with masking tape. All together, this took some time, but I felt confident that the lines would not separate during the re-rigging. As it turned out, none did.

Good luck with this, and enjoy the reward — enjoyable single-handed sailing with a lot more time spent in the cockpit and a lot less time spent on deck.

Chapter Five
Converting a Traveler to Line Control

Converting the traveler from a track with pull stops to a line control system (Fig. 1) was one of those rare projects that defied the norm — it was easy to accomplish and, when completed, worked as smoothly and predictably as if it had been installed at the boatyard.

Similar to the reason for leading lines aft, converting a traveler to a line control system satisfies the concerns of both safety and convenience; single-handed sailing becomes much more of a pleasure. Since the traveler is located either in, just forward or just aft of the cockpit, the prospect of leaving the cockpit to adjust the position of the boom is not the issue. The real issue is the frequency with which the adjustment is made.

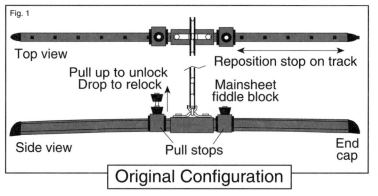

Fig. 1

Top view

Reposition stop on track

Pull up to unlock
Drop to relock

Mainsheet
fiddle block

Side view

Pull stops

End cap

Original Configuration

When the topic of line control travelers is raised, many skippers appear to be confused for one of two reasons — either they have used nothing else and so have no point of comparison, or they have never used a line control system and therefore don't know what they're missing. Often referred to as a "windward sheeting system," a line control traveler provides a mechanical advantage when adjusting the position of the boom relative to the centerline of the boat. This mechanical advantage is such that, whether on a beat or a reach, the mainsail can easily be moved to any point on the traveler. Most importantly, this can be accomplished with far less effort than would otherwise be needed. In fact, in winds over fifteen knots, coming head-to-wind is typically the only method that will decrease the pressure on the mainsail sufficiently to allow the leeward pull stop on the track to be moved. This procedure is hard on sails, reduces boat speed, and poses the risk of getting a finger caught between the pull stop and the traveler car. All of these issues, however, can be avoided when a line control traveler system is installed.

To bring the boom closer inward with a line control system, uncleat the leeward line and then pull on the windward line. With the boom in the new position, set the windward line into its cam cleat and you're finished — and of all this while still maintaining course and speed! Since it is so easy to alter the position of the boom with this system, you will likely do it more often in order to achieve the best sail trim. To place the boom in a more outboard position, uncleat the windward line and simply allow the wind to push the mainsail away from the centerline of the boat, then recleat the line.

When contemplating a traveler conversion, two options present themselves: Replace everything or modify the existing system. I have found a nearly even split between those who have elected to replace the entire system and those who choose to modify existing gear. One of the primary reasons given for a complete overhaul is that a change in location is often desired, usually to the cabin top from the cockpit. Typically this means that the old track cannot be used due to curvature, length or track size; it is quite common to find a more robust track required for a cabin top installation due to the increased loads at a mid-boom attachment point. Other considerations might include the possibility that the original equipment manufacturer is no longer in business, that a general upgrade of all systems from a different supplier is preferred or that a makeover will take advantage of recent technology. In some instances, a manufacturer's "kit" may be an attractive option.

Whatever your choice, there are several sources that can provide complete solutions. If your personal "kit" is comprised of components from several manufacturers, the total cost is likely to be less than from a single supplier. This mix-and-match alternative can result in a reliable system, provided you are more concerned with functionality and less concerned about manufacturer brand names and the appearance of matched components.

Many people prefer to maintain a piece of equipment in its original form and appearance whenever possible. In fact, I agree that there is something special about an older boat that still looks like it did when it was first built. Because of this, and the fact that the traveler track on most late model boats is installed by the builder on the cabin top, this project for me became an exercise in modifying the existing traveler instead of replacing the entire system.

The first of these conversions was completed in 1990 aboard a 1986 O'Day 28 sloop. Since the supplier of the traveler was and is still in business, information was readily available to explain how to (1) convert the existing system and (2) maintain an original equipment appearance. After spending a bit of telephone time with customer service in order to be certain of the components, I found the completed system less problematic, the installation faster, and the total cost far less than replacing everything and starting from scratch.

The first call to the manufacturer was to determine how to identify the traveler car and track on this boat. After comparing a few diagrams and making some simple measurements that were faxed to the vendor, the track arching above the companionway was identified. The maker was then able to provide a list of components by part number, some of which I purchased from a mail order marine supplier, while others were bought direct from the manufacturer. The good news was that once the installation had begun, nothing was found missing — all fasteners and other components were on hand thanks to the vendor.

The precise components needed for any traveler conversion will vary with the manufacturer, but the same basic list would include:

1. A replacement traveler car with ball bearings, if the original was not so equipped

2. Two single sheave traveler blocks with an eye strap, port and starboard
3. Two double sheave end blocks, port and starboard
4. 25 feet of ⁵⁄₁₆" line, one for port and another starboard (often one red and one green, but many prefer a single color code to identify both)

Note: Some systems are designed with only an eye strap on each side of the traveler car and a single sheave end block; this is recommended only for boats under about 26 feet. On the other hand, some systems place a double sheave on the traveler car and a triple set of sheaves on the end block. These beefier systems are required for the larger mainsails found on bigger boats and, as might be expected, the cost is proportionately higher.

Regardless of brand or model, the components of most vendors can be purchased from a local chandlery or marine mail order supplier. If replacement traveler track is necessary, it is often easier to purchase it locally than to deal with a large, unwieldy delivery. Occasionally, a manufacturer will provide some parts only on a direct basis, or will drop-ship to the end-user after the purchase has been made through a traditional retail outlet.

Since the traveler track in this particular installation was already mounted on pads and spanned the companionway directly beneath the center of the boom, the issue of track replacement was thankfully avoided. This resulted in a simpler, less time-consuming conversion and eliminated the issue of drilling the new track to match existing bolt holes or, even worse, having to fill existing holes and locate new ones. The hardware installation required only a few hours from start to finish, and the entire project could have been completed in even less time had bowline knots been used to attach the control lines to the traveler car eye straps instead of eye splices.

I use eye splices whenever possible for both strength and appearance. There have been many studies comparing the breaking strength of unmodified line, spliced line and rope tied with different types of knots. In every case, the knot that preserved the highest degree of breaking strength was a bowline but, in every case, an eye splice preserved even more. The loads on traveler lines are potentially so great during an uncontrolled jibe or at extreme angles of heel, that I prefer to provide myself with every possible advantage.

Regarding appearance, it is my opinion that eye splices lend a distinctive, finished look to any connection of line and equipment. Splicing line is a skill that many skippers have never learned. Yet it is a fundamental aspect of preparing any rope to withstand the worst, allowing the line to retain the greatest percentage of its original strength. In addition to traveler lines, splices look great on vangs, docklines, any becket or the clew of a sail.

Anyway, the installation and conversion procedure is straightforward enough. Remove the fastener from each of the two trim caps (Fig. 2) on the ends of the traveler track — if they exist — and set them aside. Next, remove both of the pull stops from the track along with the traveler car; from now on, the pull stops will make interesting paperweights but will be useful for little else. It will be necessary to remove the split ring and clevis pin from the becket that connects the mainsheet fiddle block to the traveler car in order to separate the two. The reason for this disassembly is twofold: (1) to make it easier to handle the traveler car without interference from the mainsheet lines and (2) to allow the installation of a stand-up spring on the mainsheet fiddle becket.

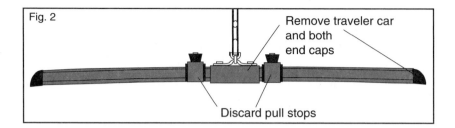

Fig. 2

Remove traveler car and both end caps

Discard pull stops

If the existing traveler car can be used, the conversion kit for it is usually quite obvious. The only parts from the original car not typically used are the two original bolts and nuts that fastened an eye strap to which the mainsheet becket was attached. I began by removing these two bolts (Fig. 3a). *Note: A ball bearing traveler car is absolutely necessary for smooth, reliable operation due to the enormous potential strain on the system when adjusting the car under load. Often, a traveler car designed specifically for a line control system will have six or more load bearing wheels.*

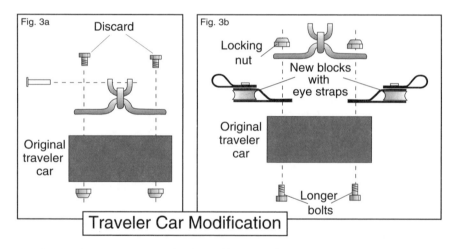

Fig. 3a

Discard

Original traveler car

Fig. 3b

Locking nut

New blocks with eye straps

Original traveler car

Longer bolts

Traveler Car Modification

The traveler car conversion kit (Fig. 3b) assembles in moments by inserting the new, longer bolts from the underside of the car, through the supplied stainless sleeves and plastic sheaves, continuing through the block mounting plate and then finally through the holes on the eye strap. Be certain the original rubber stopper is in place under the eye strap or, at the very least a toothed washer, and then tighten down the entire assembly with lock nuts and split washers. To add a touch of security, I always dip fasteners in clear silicone sealant prior to attachment. The sealant prevents the screw from backing out accidentally, but still allows intentional removal without the complications of a locking adhesive. I found this conversion kit to be quite similar to those supplied by other manufacturers; the details may differ, but the basic components and general procedure are the same.

If you plan to attach control lines to the eye straps with splices, I suggest making the splices prior to the final assembly of the traveler car. If you are using bowlines to attach the control lines to the eye straps on the traveler car, the car can now be slid back onto

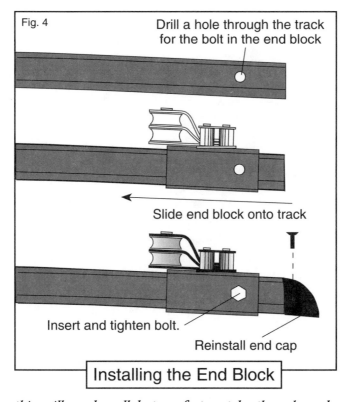

Fig. 4

Drill a hole through the track for the bolt in the end block

Slide end block onto track

Insert and tighten bolt.

Reinstall end cap

Installing the End Block

the track, followed by the end blocks and the track end caps.

Note: On some recent systems, there is no eye strap on the traveler car for the attachment of a knot or splice. On these cars, the attachment point is often accomplished by means of a metal sleeve surrounding the end of the line. This is then inserted into a hole on each side of the car, and a setscrew is tightened down to hold the line in place. In average conditions this will work well but, unfortunately, there have been more than a few instances of the control line pulling free of the traveler car. If you install one of these systems, it might be prudent to consider adding an eye strap to each side of the car in order to provide a more secure attachment point for the line. This design works well under most conditions due to its mechanical advantage, which removes much of the strain from this weak point. These systems typically have a double sheave on the traveler car and a triple on the end block providing a 6:1 mechanical advantage.

Usually, a single horizontal fore-and-aft aligned bolt and lock nut holds each of the end blocks in place. Sometimes, one or more vertically positioned bolts will terminate in the track itself with the head of the fastener ultimately made flush with the top surface of the block. In either case, an appropriate hole (Fig. 4) must be drilled to accommodate the fastener. This method of mounting the end blocks is one of the differences between a retrofit and some replacement systems. Many of the complete systems will fasten the end blocks onto the track by using one or more of the bolts that attach the track itself to the deck.

Be very careful when lining up the end blocks prior to drilling a hole through each end of the track; the old adage of measure twice and cut once is no less true here than elsewhere. During the alignment process, the end blocks have a tendency to move, and misalignment of the drilled hole is often the result. Place the head of the bolt on the aft side of the track. Apply a sealant, if desired, and tighten down each bolt with a locking nut to complete the installation of the end blocks (Fig. 5).

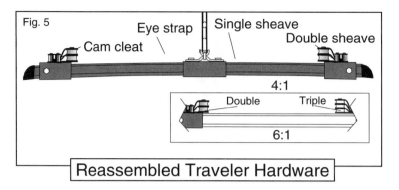

Fig. 5

Cam cleat
Eye strap
Single sheave
Double sheave

4:1

Double
Triple

6:1

Reassembled Traveler Hardware

When you reinstall the mainsheet fiddle block on the traveler car, take the opportunity to also install a standup spring (if it doesn't already have one); this will keep the fiddle off the deck when the lines are not taut. Reinsert the clevis pin through the bracket on the fiddle block, then the split ring through the pin. If the becket on the mainsheet fiddle block has no clevis pin or other closure safety mechanism, you would be well advised to replace what is there.

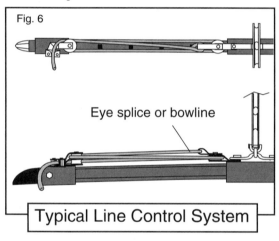

Fig. 6

Eye splice or bowline

Typical Line Control System

The final operation is to reeve the control lines through the blocks (Fig. 6) so they exit the cam cleats properly aft. This conversion kit provided a fixed cam cleat on each end block; on some systems, this would be a pivoting cam cleat instead. If the traveler is placed well forward of the companionway or a spray dodger, it might be more convenient to remove the cam cleats from the end blocks and install them on the cabin top near the cockpit. If the cleats on the end blocks do not lend themselves to reinstallation, replacement models are available, in either fixed or swivel versions, for mounting on the cabin top.

If you single-hand sail more often than not, then this traveler system conversion will feel similar to going from an automobile with a manual transmission to one with an automatic. In addition to ease of use, mainsail trim becomes more accurate simply because the operation is so easily accomplished; since adjustments in trim are so easy to do, you will make them more often. With 25 feet of line on each end of the traveler, the mainsail can be trimmed as readily as the jib while you remain at the helm. If you choose to make this modification, you will likely have a warm fuzzy and a smile from the very first use.

Chapter Six
The Great Cover-up

If you have spent even a few hours aboard a boat in Texas during the summer, you know how hot it can be out on the water! It is the unfortunate crew indeed that departs the dock for even a daysail without some means of protection from the sun. And, almost without exception, that protection takes the form of a canvas-covered metal frame.

The variety of shape, size and color for a sun protector is incredibly diverse; a skipper's imagination and budget are the only limiting factors. If you have been around boats for many years, you are no doubt familiar with many of the ways in which shade can be provided, both while under way and at anchor. If you are new to boating, however, the terminology and options might be confusing.

In addition to broad sweeps of shade, there is a seemingly endless variety of accessory items that can also be made from canvas. Often, simply becoming aware that such choices exist is the first step towards solving problems and protecting yourself or valuable equipment from the sun's ultraviolet rays. Let's begin with the fabrics themselves.

Fabric overview

Although usually referred to as "canvas," many special fabrics developed for marine applications are manufactured from synthetic materials known as acrylics. Since these fabrics, as a group, have an appearance and feel similar to that of cotton canvas, they are referred to as canvas in almost any discussion relative to shade protection and equipment covers.

There are two primary registered trade names for this type of material, Sunbrella made by Glen Raven Mills, and Diklon 32 from Dickson Elberton Mills. The most commonly heard name is that of Sunbrella and, for purposes of clarity, I will refer to this type of material as Sunbrella or simply as canvas. These fabrics have several properties that lend themselves to marine use, namely durability of color, ultraviolet and mildew resistance, limited stretch and a water-repellent surface. This last item is perhaps one of the most important reasons why these fabrics are so popular for use on boats.

An alternative to canvas is vinyl-coated polyester. This fabric is a good choice for applications in which regular cleaning would be difficult — the top of a flybridge bimini, for example. Vinyl-coated polyester will not last as long as canvas, however, and offers fewer color options.

Sunbrella is available in solids, stripes and prints, with solid colors being the most common choice for boats. Striped canvas is not often used for sunshades due to a limited number of colors and the difficulty of lining up stripe patterns with the seams and edges of the finished product. In general, prints are reserved for cushions, pillows, curtains and other interior items.

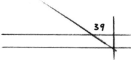

The durability of canvas in exposed applications is excellent — the manufacturers provide a five-year warranty against color fading, with a life expectancy of ten years or more if cared for properly.

In a number of instances, canvas represents only a portion of the complete product. For many installations, clear vinyl will also be used and, as you might expect, this material is available in several levels of quality. The determining factors here are clarity, flexibility, thickness and surface finish. The most desirable combination generally comes in the form of a forty-gauge vinyl sheet that is double polished; it has the greatest degree of clarity, and the surface is identical on both sides. And, because it is fairly thick, it can be made flexible enough to withstand a fair degree of abuse over a long period of time. Since continuous prolonged exposure to the sun will cause the vinyl to turn yellow and cloudy, clear vinyl panels are often supplied with removable canvas covers. If left unprotected, clear vinyl will eventually crack and split from ultraviolet damage.

Recent years have seen the introduction of a material made from polycarbonate, which provides virtually the same clarity as glass. Known by a variety of trade names including Lexan, this flexible transparent material is ideal for applications in which clarity is the primary concern and cost is not.

Most enclosures are constructed using a variety of materials including, on occasion, this flexible polycarbonate material. It is not uncommon for a conventional enclosure to also have a Lexan panel just forward of the helm or in the center of a large windshield. Lexan can be sewn into the center panel in the same manner as vinyl, along with a zipper. The primary difference, aside from cost, is that this material cannot be rolled up but, instead, must be hinged in order to be moved out of the way. When a hardtop is present, Lexan is attached along the upper edge of the panel.

Another fabric often found attached to canvas products is a mesh that is available from several manufacturers, the most common of which is called Textilene. This synthetic material is UV-, mildew- and fade-resistant. It can shade most of the sun's heat and still allow a breeze to penetrate, but is available in only a limited number of colors. There is some visibility through the material, although to a far lesser degree than clear vinyl.

Yet another fabric is mosquito screen. As you might guess, this is an excellent warm weather option for enclosures that encompass the entire cockpit or flybridge. The advantage of this material is obvious, but keep in mind that a finer screen will also block more breezes along with smaller insects. Netting is produced in even fewer colors than Textilene, and can be made to zip into place or to assemble with Velcro or a similar closure.

Cleaning and maintenance

Although extremely durable, both canvas and vinyl require regular care in order to provide the life expectancy and usefulness demanded of these products. In general, canvas should be rinsed as often as you rinse your boat. Mildew can only grow where dirt exists, and this simple activity will get rid of most of the dirt, pollution and salt that can accumulate.

According to Glen Raven Mills, the combination of four ounces of Ivory Soap and four ounces of bleach in a gallon of water is the ideal cleaning agent for canvas. As an alternative, almost any properly diluted biodegradable general-purpose cleaner can be used; a thorough rinse should follow either method. *Note: For small canvas items, a washing machine is an option, but under no circumstances should a dryer be used. All items must be air dried in order to avoid shrinkage.*

In addition to regular cleaning, make sure the waterproofing is renewed about every three years: Remove the canvas, and clean both sides. Allow it to air dry, then apply a silicone-based waterproofing agent. For this or any marine fabric application, avoid solutions such as Thompson Water Seal. Wood sealers are made to soak into the material instead of remaining on the surface. The canvas should be waterproofed again annually, beginning at year four.

As for clear vinyl, the care and feeding of this material is very different. Since vinyl is soft as well as transparent, any cleaner with an abrasive will scratch the surface, reducing its clarity. Cleaners such as Sof-Scrub, although excellent for some purposes, will quickly destroy the visibility of vinyl. Some of the recommended cleaners for clear vinyl are 303 Protectant, Armor-All, Lemon Pledge and Plexus Vinyl cleaner; of these, Plexus is mentioned most often. Apply these cleaners using a clean, soft cloth — a cotton diaper is ideal. If you rinse this material frequently and clean it regularly, your clear vinyl will likely last for many years. *Note: Buy your cleaners carefully. Even though a product may be free of abrasives, if it contains bleach or phosphates, it will eventually damage your vinyl.*

If the canvas or vinyl item has zippers, a regular application of silicone or petroleum jelly will help ensure smooth operation. A friend of mine swears that Chap Stick contains UV inhibitors that will successfully keep zippers running smooth. These same lubricants should be applied to snaps and snap posts to assure trouble-free removal and replacement of hardware.

With only a little extra care, the life expectancy of canvas products can be increased significantly. Whereas some biminis last three years, others last ten; the difference is simply a matter of care by the owner. Longevity can be summarized pretty simply: Most everyone asks about it; some people think about it; most don't do it. It's not much fun, but proper care and maintenance does make a tremendous difference.

The details

Regardless of the canvas product, many aspects of materials, workmanship and business operations are common among the best of canvas vendors. The guide below lists some of the most important details. Use this information to help guarantee that you receive the best value and design possible.

1. **Insurance.** Be certain that the canvas provider you have chosen has obtained the appropriate liability insurance. If a contractor boards your boat and causes an accident or damage, you are liable if he or she is uninsured. This is true of work performed by any contractor.

2. **Length of time in operation.** A warranty is of no value if the company that

offers it goes out of business. Most reputable canvas shops, at least on the Gulf Coast, have been in business long enough to have replaced canvas several times for the same owner. In some cases, a shop may have made several "suits" of canvas for a boat that has traded hands several times.

3. **Custom fit.** The item should be measured *aboard* your boat, and should be made specifically for it. Many companies offer products created from patterns that are generally correct for your boat make, model and length, but not exact. For the best combination of attractive appearance and optimum function, nothing can beat a custom fit regardless of the product.

4. **Reinforced seams.** In addition to looking good, the product should last for years. Ideally, the raw edge should be placed inside a seam that has been folded at least twice.

5. **Type of thread.** Polyester thread that is UV resistant is best. In years past, this was available only in white, but additional colors have recently come on the market. If your canvas shop continues to use only white, it's probably because colored threads still tend to fade to white.

6. **Stainless steel.** The thickness of the metal wall can make a big difference in the strength of the finished product. Of course, there are different qualities of stainless steel. Virtually all frames are made from ⅞" or 1" stainless steel tubing of "good" quality. An alternative to stainless steel is chrome-plated steel, which offers the same strength as stainless, is less expensive but more prone to discoloration. *Note: Although aluminum frames can indeed be made, the life expectancy of aluminum is far shorter and its strength far less. None of the canvas shops I interviewed will build a frame of aluminum, even at the insistence of the client.*

7. **Mounting hardware.** Stainless frames can be installed either on the deck or on the stainless steel tubing of a stern pulpit. If hardware is attached to fiberglass, silicone is used to seal the holes and yet allow easy removal of the fitting should the need arise. Use mounting hardware made only of stainless steel. Among vendors, there seems to be some difference of opinion as to whether or not the tubing should be drilled and tapped for screws that fasten the fittings to the tubing. In most cases, holes are drilled and tapped with threads only for large screws on primary fittings. Where setscrews are installed, the tubing is often merely "dimpled" with a center punch. None of the shops interviewed expressed a perceived need to seal any of the screws with Loctite or a similar material.

8. **Zippers.** They should be UV- and rust-resistant (not metal), easy to operate and somewhat large. If they are found on the top or exterior of the product, zippers should be covered when possible to prevent premature deterioration.

9. **Tie downs.** If you use straps to tension the frame, make sure they are made of nylon. This material appears to be more UV-resistant and colorfast than cotton webbing or polyester. Stainless steel D-rings are considered the best choice for hardware on these straps.

10. **Extras.** There are numerous trim and appearance options — piping, a contrasting fabric stripe or a window, to name a few. Personal taste and budget reign supreme.

11. **Samples.** A good canvas shop will be eager to show off their work. Although some product samples will be available at the vendor's place of business, taking a look at clients' boats will provide a better feel for the quality of custom work the vendor can provide. Examination of installed products will no doubt also generate ideas for your own boat.

Applications

When talking with canvas shop owners, a recurring concern presented itself regarding first-time boat owners. It is common, it seems, for a new boat owner to not only be confused about the names of various products, but also to be largely uninformed regarding the vast array of products and options available. Some skippers use canvas products on only a minimal basis, while others literally cover their boat from stem to stern.

I encourage new boat owners to use their vessel for a while before making decisions regarding major canvas items. Until you've spent some time on board, it's pretty tough to know exactly what you want.

As previously mentioned, the issues of protection and convenience are the primary reasons for installing canvas products. To many boat owners, an even greater concern is the issue of maintenance avoidance. For instance, canvas covers made for exterior varnished woods will indefinitely postpone costly refinishing, and covers for metal air horns can prevent the need for frequent polishing.

Unfortunately, many skippers are under the mistaken impression that canvas covers eliminate the need for *any* maintenance, but this is simply not the case. In truth, fabric covers can often mask problems that developed as a result of insufficient maintenance. Trapped moisture can cause discoloration of stainless steel; "permanent" hatch covers can trap salts that will pit an aluminum frame; and even a covered dinghy in davits needs uncovering and washing occasionally.

Although canvas items for powerboats and sailboats have similarities, enough differences exist to require separate treatment.

Dodgers. A dodger, usually referred to as a "spray dodger," protects the cockpit and its occupants from salt spray and wind coming over the bow. Typically spanning the cabin top just forward of the companionway, a dodger sweeps in a curve towards the forward ends of the coaming on both sides of the cockpit (Fig. 1). This structure is rarely taller than five feet or so from the floor of the cockpit; often, it is much shorter. Used primarily in the winter to deflect the cold or while at sea in any weather, a dodger provides little in the way of overhead shade.

Most canvas and upholstery vendors recommend dodgers primarily for boats that are going offshore. Often, less expensive options exist if daysailing or coastal cruising is the main activity.

A dodger can be as small as the companionway opening itself or as large as the entire beam of the boat. A dodger is a combination of canvas and clear vinyl, often with

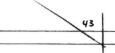

removable side panels and a roll-up front. A dodger with side panels that can be removed is often referred to as a "California" dodger. In an effort to help preserve the life of the vinyl, removable canvas covers are invariably a part of the ensemble and included in the cost; if the clear vinyl is not continuously exposed to the sun, it will last much longer.

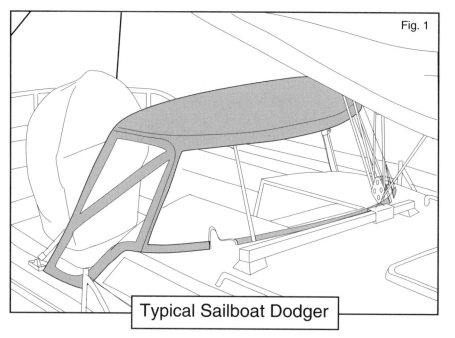

Fig. 1

Typical Sailboat Dodger

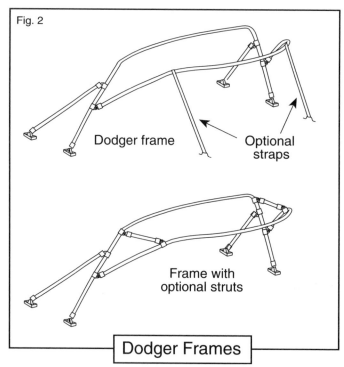

Fig. 2

Dodger frame

Optional straps

Frame with optional struts

Dodger Frames

The frame of a dodger can be a simple affair with minimal structure or it can be quite substantial with additional struts for maximum rigidity, as shown in Fig. 2. In either case, a great deal of a dodger's strength is derived from the tension of the canvas on its stainless steel frame. Ideally, a dodger should also provide a reliable grab hold for the crew.

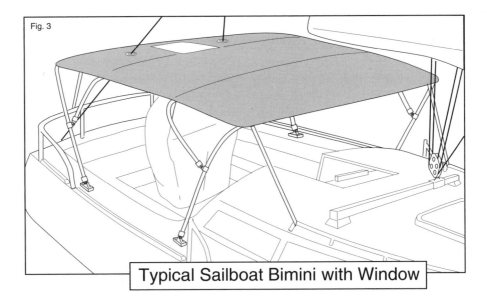

Fig. 3

Typical Sailboat Bimini with Window

In order to provide shade in addition to frontal protection, a dodger is often used in conjunction with a bimini (below). This combination has the potential to shade such a large portion of the boat that passengers may find it objectionable; it is difficult to "work on your tan" if the only place to catch rays is the foredeck.

A dodger can also be made quite small. Many cruising boats will have small dodgers on larger forward deck hatches or secondary companionways. These miniature dodgers allow airflow into the cabin, but still prevent unwanted spray from entering the opening.

Biminis. The most common design found on sailboats from thirty feet and over is a four-bow sailing bimini. This style provides easy, unobstructed access to the cockpit, substantial strength, and makes possible a larger size. The permutations on this design are almost endless: There can be a window on the top that allows a view of the mainsail and masthead; it can be made to accommodate a single or split backstay; there are a variety of removable panels from which to choose, etc.

Another option seen on an increasing number of biminis is a three-sided zippered opening between the second and third bows, which is often called a "moonroof." In addition to being able to see the stars without taking the bimini down, it also makes a

RULE of THUMB:

If the bimini top is too big for the boat, the whole vessel looks out of balance. Boats with very large cockpits may suffer a bit in appearance if the entire cockpit is shaded.

TIP:

A windshield is sometimes referred to in error as a dodger; a dodger is a free-standing structure, while a windshield is simply an option for a bimini.

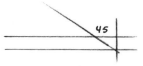

lot of sense for those really pretty days when the sun is out, but the temperature is not hot. There are limitless trim and appearance options; almost anything a boat owner can imagine can be done.

The bimini illustrated in Figure 3 is known as a sailing bimini because it can remain in place while under sail. On the other hand, a flying bimini (Fig. 4) shades the cockpit nearly as well as the standard version, but is not used while under sail due to flexing of the standing rigging. Although this movement can cause a flying bimini to come loose from its anchor points on the backstay, it is still quite useful under power.

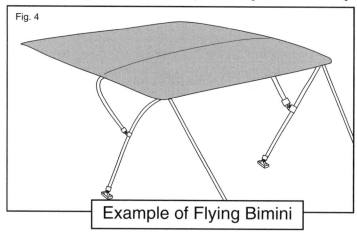

Fig. 4

Example of Flying Bimini

A flying bimini can be installed with only two front bows of stainless steel along with webbing tension straps, while the rear is usually tied to the backstays; a PVC pole is used for support across the rear edge. A flying bimini could be an option worth considering if a less expensive cockpit shade alternative is needed. Most flying biminis can be modified to accept a set of stainless rear bows at some future date, ultimately creating a standard sailing bimini.

There are three primary forms of free-standing bimini frames (Fig. 5) made from stainless steel. The three-bow design is the least stable, and does not provide as secure a place to grab if the going gets rough. In addition, the attachment point for a three-bow frame will almost always interfere with the most convenient boarding area. On smaller boats this may be unavoidable, but on larger vessels a three-bow frame is not a wise choice.

One of the main reasons for using stainless steel tubing for bimini frames rather than aluminum is the fit. You can't stretch the canvas as tight on an aluminum frame, and the fabric wears out quicker if it flaps around.

Many skippers don't want to be bothered with details, taking the position of "just build me a top and be sure it's a good one." The two main factors to consider when making a "good" bimini top are style and function.

TIP:

The smaller the weave of the mesh, the more effective it will be at keeping out insects. However, as the mesh becomes tighter, airflow decreases; at some point, insufficient airflow could negate the benefit of the insect barrier.

A bimini top needs to complement the boat. You have to be able to operate the winches and, of course, you have to be able to get on and off the boat without having to crawl around the frame.

Most installations are of the four-bow variety; it is not uncommon, however, to find five-bow frames on the largest boats.

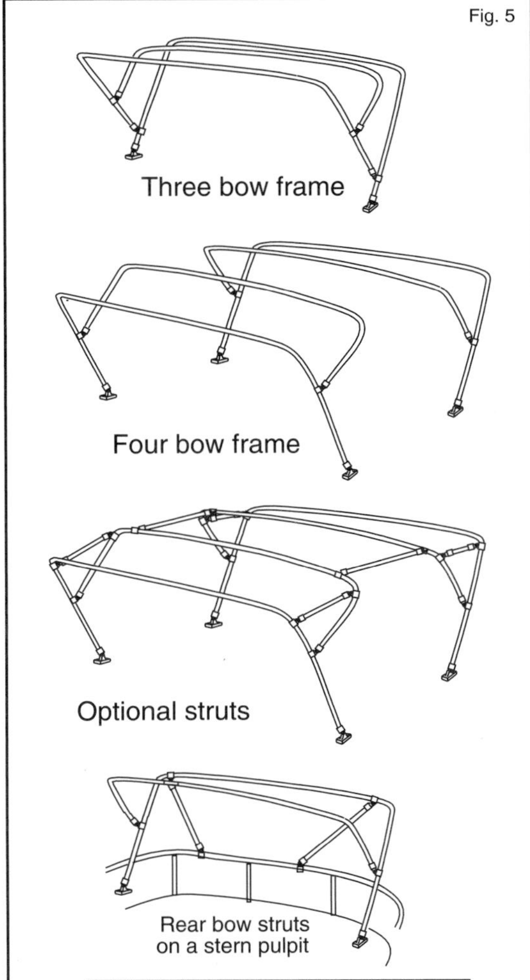

Fig. 5

Three bow frame

Four bow frame

Optional struts

Rear bow struts
on a stern pulpit

Typical Bimini Frames

Please note that optional struts (Fig. 5) can be added — all or in part — to produce a frame that is extremely rigid. It is also common to find struts used vertically to help stabilize larger frames. This can be seen in the form of supports attached to the stern pulpit, the transom, the swim platform or even the hull sides. And, as you might expect, the cost rises proportionately with each added pair of struts.

Regardless of the type of bimini or the number of bows, many options exist in the form of vertical panels. These panels can be added in order to increase the amount of shade provided, to further protect the cockpit or to increase the "living" space aboard. Figure 6 illustrates some of the more common additions to a free-standing bimini, as follows:

Bimini A shows a Textilene panel that has been added to one side. Often, a single panel can be used either port or starboard, wherever it is most needed. It is fastened with a zipper across the top and several grommets along the bottom that have light line or shock cord attached. Front panels are also often used to protect the cockpit from the sun's heat, while still allowing a breeze to penetrate the mesh.

Bimini B illustrates a windshield, sometimes called a "front enclosure." This is made up of as many as three clear vinyl panels that have been zipped together vertically, as well as across the top.

Bimini C is an example of a full enclosure. As its name implies, the entire cockpit is

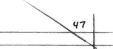

surrounded by zippered panels that completely enclose the cockpit. These panels are most often made of clear vinyl designed to increase the air-conditioned space in the summer as well as keep out the cold in winter. Enclosures can also be made of mesh or mosquito netting; it is not uncommon to find complete sets of panels made from different materials.

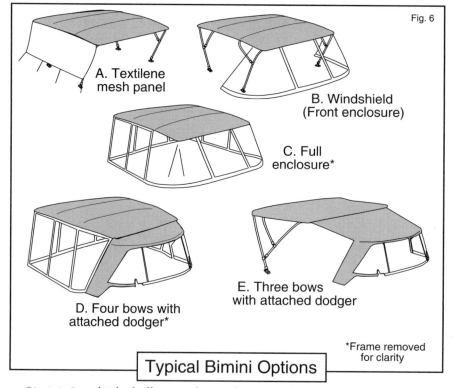

Fig. 6

A. Textilene mesh panel

B. Windshield (Front enclosure)

C. Full enclosure*

D. Four bows with attached dodger*

E. Three bows with attached dodger

*Frame removed for clarity

Typical Bimini Options

Biminis D and E both illustrate the combination of a bimini connected to a spray dodger. Bimini D is a four-bow design with a full enclosure; bimini E is a three-bow model left open on three sides. In both cases, the panel that connects the bimini to the dodger can be made of either canvas or vinyl, depending upon the size of the space between the two and the forward visibility desired.

Awnings. Whether used alone or in addition to a dodger and bimini, awnings provide the most effective means of creating large areas of shade. Awnings are typically erected only while in a slip, at a mooring or at anchor. (They limit visibility and require the halyards to lift the awning into position.)

All awnings fall into one of two broad categories — structured or unstructured. Structured awnings are usually supported by means of athwartships PVC poles that have been capped (Fig. 7). These poles, usually 1½" in diameter, are slid into long tube-like pockets sewn across the ends of the awning both fore and aft. Sometimes, a tube is sewn across the middle as well. A light line is then rigged from each corner to the center, along with an additional line that lifts the center of the fabric. All of these lines are then shackled to a halyard, and the entire assembly is lifted to a position that is several feet above the deck. To complete the installation, the corners and edges are tied to lifelines and stanchions at several points.

Figure 7 depicts the usual arrangement of two awnings, one for the foredeck and another aft of the mast; the forward awning is held aloft by a second jib halyard while the awning aft is held up by the main halyard. On a ketch-rigged boat, the mizzen halyard could be used to hoist a third awning over the aft deck.

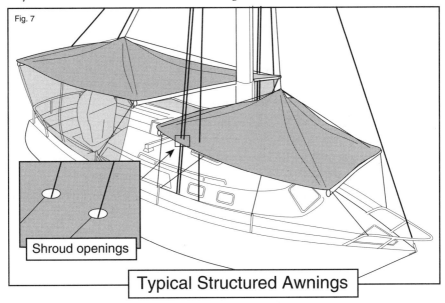

Fig. 7

Shroud openings

Typical Structured Awnings

One aspect of awning design that can substantially affect the price involves openings for the rigging. If you desire full awning coverage, you must allow for (1) the placement of shrouds and (2) mainsail flaking systems, such as a Dutchman or Lazy Jacks. This is accomplished most often with round openings that are zippered or closed with Velcro (Fig. 7 inset) after the awning has been set into place; both forward and aft awnings may require this attention. The additional labor required to create multiple small openings in the correct strategic locations can add significantly to the overall cost of an awning. The result, however, is a custom fit that provides the greatest amount of shade.

Although awnings are made most often from canvas, contractors sometimes use vinyl-coated polyester or cotton/polyester. Disposable plastic tarps are also an alternative, but plastic tarps are never used by quality-conscious canvas shops to make awnings. At best, they are a very low-cost, temporary alternative.

Structured awnings — those with athwartships supporting poles — offer several advantages over those without rigid supporting members.

They can:
- be positioned higher off the deck,

TIP:

Because awnings require such large amounts of fabric, awnings are sometimes just as costly as shade products made with stainless steel tubing, such as biminis.

- be made with interchangeable side panels,
- offer greater protection from the weather, and are more likely to survive a storm.

Regarding your expenditure, if ultimate cost is an important part of your thinking, more money spent at the beginning may prove a better bargain over time. An awning is often more durable if it is made with properly installed support poles.

The PVC poles installed with structured awnings are long, and they bend. This means that the pole ends should not be tied tightly, but instead left slack, allowing the poles to flex. Some skippers insist on pulling the tie-downs tight, resulting in poles that are permanently bent in a downward curve from the tension of the lines and the heat of the sun. If you tie them loosely and allow the entire assembly to flex with the weather, the poles will remain relatively straight for many years.

An important disadvantage of structured awnings, other than cost, is the issue of storage. Although space can often be found for the fabric, several PVC poles that are eight to ten feet in length can present a storage challenge. As a lesser issue, more time is required to remove and replace an awning made with poles than one made without. And, of course, a pole-less awning will be less costly to make.

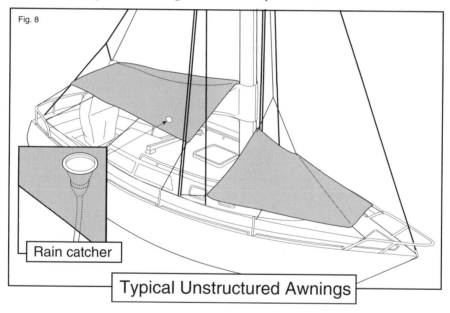

Fig. 8

Rain catcher

Typical Unstructured Awnings

Unstructured awnings offer many skippers an alternative that may be preferable. There are still two pieces required for full coverage (Fig. 8), but in many cases the shrouds are simply avoided, leaving some portions of the deck unshaded. If full coverage is desired, customary openings can be made to accommodate the shrouds.

If a flaking system is present, many people find it easier to assemble and remove an awning without poles. For instance, if a Dutchman flaking system is present, the vertical lines woven into the sail can be easily dealt with — if the awning draped across the boom has been made in two sections that snap, tie or Velcro together along the length of the mainsail. The edges can then be tied to the lifelines and stanchions as usual.

Whether structured or not, all awnings can be fitted with options such as a window or raincatcher (Fig. 8 inset). A window in an awning is similar to a window in a bimini; a raincatcher is uncommon except for awnings.

A raincatcher is a round opening in the awning to which a valve and tubing are attached. This opening is most commonly several inches across and made of plastic or stainless. In practice, rainwater is directed through the tubing to buckets or bladders for later use in showers and dishwashing.

Accessories

Most of the items listed here are fairly inexpensive. Collectively, they will enhance the appearance of the boat, protect the item covered and reduce maintenance. Most of these

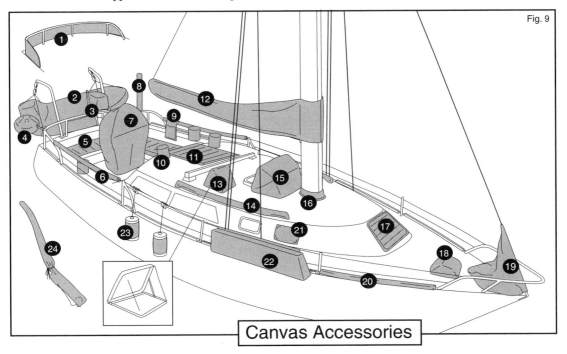

Fig. 9

Canvas Accessories

items will be familiar to an experienced sailor, but this may be an introduction to the new boat owner. Let's begin at the transom and move forward, starting with the stern pulpit.

The stern rail can be the location of **weather clothes** (#1), designed to surround the cockpit for an additional margin of safety. Made with Sunbrella or a similar acrylic marine "canvas," weather clothes fasten to the rails with turn locks, snaps or ties, and will help to keep the sea out and boat stuff on board. Weather clothes can also be made of wood, fiberglass or opaque Plexiglas.

Whether rigid or inflatable, a dinghy will always benefit from a **canvas dinghy cover** (#2). The cover can enclose just the hull, or may also cover the motor. A well-made cover will allow airflow beneath, to help prevent mildew. If the outboard motor is stored separate from the dinghy, a **motor cover** (#3) will help to prolong the motor's appearance.

Although made from excellent quality stainless steel, a grill (#4) will remain more

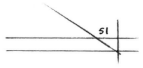

attractive if covered. **Grill covers** are usually made with a drawstring and, often, piping or some other trim in a contrasting color.

If you have spent much time in the cockpit, you have experienced the discomfort of unadorned seating. **Cockpit cushions** (#5) can make any activity in the cockpit much more enjoyable. Made from vinyl or canvas fabric, cushions not only provide a more comfortable seat, they also can add to the appearance of the boat.

Cockpit cushions contain either open-cell or closed-cell foam. Open-cell foam is softer but will retain water; closed-cell foam is more rigid but can be soaked with water and not get soggy. In appearance, cushions can be quilted, multi-colored and shaped to precisely fit the contours of the cockpit. A good quality set of cushions will last for many years.

You may be surprised to discover the existence of **lifeline cushions** (#6). Since leaning back against a lifeline is not terribly comfortable, many people opt for tubular cushions made in six-foot lengths. These are available in most well-stocked marine stores and, although functional, are not very attractive. Color-coordinated covers for these foam tubes prolong the life of the foam and look more attractive than bare foam.

A **wheel bag** (#7) can cover the steering wheel and everything else that has been installed on the pedestal — an inexpensive way to protect many items at once. Made to accommodate just the steering wheel or an entire console, a wheel bag will prolong the life of a leather wheel cover, the liquid in a compass and the LCD display of many instruments.

Covers come in many forms, and are made for many applications. Sometimes canvas is used to cover and protect other fabric products. A **flagstaff cover** (#8) will shield an expensive flag and its teak staff for a fraction of the replacement cost of either item.

A sailboat has many lines leading to the cockpit and, in an effort to sort out the confusion, many skippers choose to install **line bags**. These wide, flat pouches can be made to hang from a lifeline (#9) or they can attach to the cockpit bulkhead. In either case, the closure is usually elastic and the pouch can be made in any one of many colors.

Although good quality winches will last for many years even if exposed to the elements, **winch covers** (#10) can protect the finish and reduce the frequency of polishing. Most winch covers have an elastic band sewn into an interior collar, keeping the cover in place even in high winds.

Whether in the heat of the summer or the cold of winter, a **quilted companionway cover** (#11) will help to insulate the cabin. These quilted covers contain insulating material, snap in place, and are made to cover the drop boards as well as the companionway hatch. Some skippers even have the name of the boat stitched to the cover.

The most common of all canvas covers on a sailboat is a **mainsail cover** (#12). These can be made to cover just the sail and boom, or may also accommodate a rigid vang and blocks at the base of the mast. A mainsail cover can have the boat name stitched in place or contrasting piping; for that matter, it can be made of

striped canvas. If a sail flaking system is present, the design of the cover will always accommodate the particulars of the system.

In milder weather, a mosquito net **"tent"** (#13) can be an effective means of providing some airflow while keeping pests outside. The tents are dropped over an open hatch (#13 inset); lead shot sewn into the perimeter of the bottom seam holds the netting in place. A tent may be made to fit any size hatch or, for that matter, any size anything. (One canvas shop that I know of has developed a one-piece tent that can be dropped over a bimini top!) There are no zippers or panels, and the bottom is weighted to keep the lower edge on the deck. It looks a bit odd at first glance, but it appears to work.

One of the best ways to postpone wood refinishing indefinitely is to cover brightwork with canvas. The **grab rails on deck** (#14) are a good example. These covers have snaps located between the feet of a grab rail and, in some instances, are also held in place with a snap at each end of the cover. (In this case, one half of the fastener is attached to the grab rail itself.)

Similar to spray dodgers for the cockpit are **hatch dodgers** (#15) on the cabin top. Don't overlook this option if you have a secondary crew entrance or a very large forward hatch. Customarily, in order to preserve visibility from the cockpit, a hatch dodger will be no wider than the opening it surrounds, and no taller than a couple of feet. It might be made in the same fashion as a cockpit dodger — canvas on a tubular frame — but often is simply a shaped canvas tent that fits over the open hatch and snaps in place to the deck.

Even though an effective weather seal has been installed at the base of the mast, a **mast boot cover** (#16) is invariably more attractive. With a string, or hook and loop closure around the top and bottom of the cover, a mast boot cover will add to your boat's appearance, and should remain in place regardless of the weather.

Similar to an insulated, quilted companionway cover, **hatch covers** (#17) can help to keep out extremes of heat and cold. An additional benefit of hatch covers is the preservation of the transparent portion of the hatch. Whether the "window" is made of Lexan, Plexiglas or acrylic, thousands of small cracks will eventually appear if the hatch is left unprotected against the sun. This condition is called crazing, and the only solution is to replace the window or, failing that, the entire hatch.

As mentioned several times, protection of equipment and the reduction of maintenance are two of the key reasons for canvas covers. Sometimes, a cover will be used to hide the unsightly results of normal use, and nowhere can this be more true than in the case of an **anchor windlass** (#18).

An anchor often gets rinsed after use, but rarely does a windlass. Yet the windlass will have collected salts and deposits from the rode and chain; without at least a rinse, these materials are left to destroy the finish and mechanism of the windlass. You can cover the windlass to preserve its appearance, or cover the windlass to hide its appearance. Either way, it's a good idea.

When it comes to headsails, canvas can be used in one of two ways. If the sail is of

the hank-on variety, a **sail bag** (#19) of Sunbrella keeps the sail at the ready and adds some color to the foredeck. If the sail is installed on a roller furling system, the **UV cover** will invariably be made of canvas; choose a color that contrasts with the white of the sail, but co-ordinates with the rest of the boat. The condition of the UV cover should be inspected annually for places that need to be restitched; normal use will eventually break threads on the cover.

The toe rails or caprails are often varnished, and there is no better way to protect the finish than with **canvas rail covers** (#20). These covers usually snap on the side of the gunnels and are held in place with lead weight on the outside seams. It is not uncommon to see covers of this type running the entire length of a boat, including around the stern. The covers can also be extended to fit the wood planking found on the upper portion of some hulls; examples of this type of trim are builders such as Hans Christian and Lord Nelson.

Although screens often accompany opening ports, sometimes covering the port from the outside is preferred, especially if the boat will remain unused for extended periods of time. This is easily accomplished with **snap-on canvas port covers** (#21) that are attractive and require little in the way of storage.

Most boats have cockpit cushions and, usually, two of these cushions are rather long. Designed to match the length of the cockpit, the cushions aligned fore and aft can be a storage problem. If the boat is used only on weekends, the cushions can be stored below, but where do they go if you live aboard? The answer, of course, is a **cushion storage bag**.

Made to attach to a lifeline, this **storage bag** (#22) solves many problems: It gets the cushions out of the cockpit, protects them from sun and rain, and prevents insects from entering the cabin along with stored cushions. When the cushions are in use, the bag can be easily stowed in a lazarette.

Covers for fenders (#23) not only look good, but also will prevent fenders from creating an unsightly area on the hull. These covers are available ready-made from marine retailers in several colors or from canvas shops in custom colors.

Plastics in almost any form will abrade most surfaces if left to rub against each other. When a plastic fender rubs against a plastic hull, the result is an area that must be compounded and polished in order to be restored. Much of this abrasion can be avoided if fender covers are used.

If your boat has a tiller instead of a wheel, attractive covers are made for you, too. A **canvas tiller cover** (#24) will protect the beauty of a laminated tiller almost indefinitely. To secure the cover, a tie or snap collar prevents the cover from being lost in a high wind.

Undoubtedly, there are applications for many canvas accessories that have not been mentioned here; after all, almost anything can be covered in an effort to protect whatever lies beneath.

Chapter Seven
Relocating a VHF Radio

Have you ever wondered why a VHF radio is typically mounted in the main cabin instead of on deck? After all, it's useless from the cockpit. In fact, whether sailing with crew or single-handing, the best that can be expected in the cockpit is to be able to hear someone hailing you, and usually only then if an extension speaker has been installed. On many sailboats, a radio in the cabin cannot be heard if the engine is running unless, once again, an extension speaker has been installed in the cockpit. So why do boatbuilders and skippers continue to install VHF radios in the cabin? Tradition!

O nly in the last few years have radios and other electronics been made waterproof to the degree that they could be expected to survive the harsh marine environment. And while not all marine instruments are ready for the exposure of the cockpit, many models of VHF radios are designed specifically for the rigors of salt air and sunlight.

In addition to the manufacturers' weather resistance designs, most sailboats have a canvas structure of some description that helps to protect the cockpit and everything in it — a bimini, a dodger, an awning or a combination of these. The question then becomes not if the radio should be moved to the cockpit, but where the radio should be placed. There are several choices, all of which make sense on different boats.

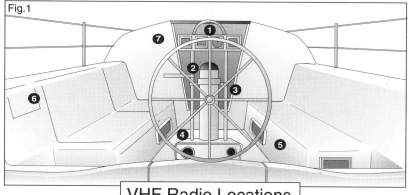

Fig.1

VHF Radio Locations

Figure 1 illustrates a typical T-shaped sailboat cockpit with a pedestal and wheel steering. This cockpit layout provides many possible locations for a radio, all of which satisfy two basic criteria — out-of-the-way, but still easily accessible. Let's review the options shown in Fig. 1. *Note: For a sailboat with a tiller, all but the locations on the pedestal still represent good choices.*

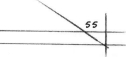

Position #1 is shown on top of the instrument pod. Almost without exception, a bracket is supplied with the radio, which can provide this option. Often, the radio has already been installed in the cabin with this bracket, so it is a simple matter to relocate the entire assembly. In fact, the same bracket is used if you choose to use any location from number one through number four.

Positions #1 and #4 (atop instrument enclosures) require only that new holes be drilled to match the holes in the brackets. Positions #2 and #3 require the purchase of an accessory arm that first attaches to the pedestal guard. If yours is an Edson pedestal, this accessory arm is readily available from marine retailers or direct from Edson. If your steering station is not an Edson, an accessory platform may still be available. The tube diameter of the guard should be one inch, and the space between the guard tubes should be nine inches on centers. If the tube diameter is close but the spacing between is not, position #3 would remain an option.

Since positions #5 (lower vertical wall of the seat), #6 (in the lid of a propane locker) and #7 (in the forward cockpit bulkhead) require that an opening be cut in the fiberglass, a flush mount kit instead of brackets will be needed to complete the installation.

For me, cutting large holes in my boat is always a scary proposition. I do it often enough, but just before I start to cut I always panic just a little. Did I measure correctly? Is this the best location? Is this the best solution? Do I really need to do this?

Just remember the old saw: Measure twice and cut once. If you have done this, you will likely have no problems with the installation.

There are two parts to this project — the installation of the radio and the rerouting of the wiring. Let's relocate the radio first.

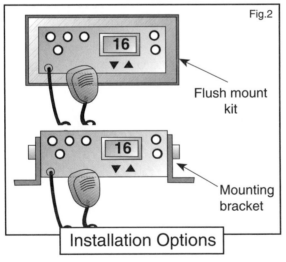

Fig.2

Flush mount kit

Mounting bracket

Installation Options

To begin, a decision must be made regarding the new location of the radio. If it is similar to any of position numbers 5 through 7, a flush mount kit (Fig.2) will be needed if the radio was not originally installed with one. This kit is a frame and bracket assembly that allows the radio to be recessed into a cutout opening.

On the other hand, if you have chosen any of the positions #1 through #4, the installation is made with the bracket that accompanied the radio when new (Fig. 2). The unit can be moved from its present location, complete with mounting hardware, to a new location with little more fuss than drilling holes for the brackets.

If you have chosen to use an accessory platform on the pedestal guard, this will need to be attached to the guard prior to mounting the radio. The only complication this

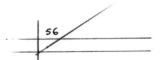

installation could present is that of adjusting the compass due to the mass of the radio and the electromagnetic field produced by the radio or any other electrical device.

Virtually all binnacle compasses are equipped with a mechanical compensation adjustment on the bottom. The compass users' manual, along with other reference books, describes this process in detail. The procedure is more time-consuming than difficult, and will result in an added benefit — you will create a deviation card that will be invaluable when going offshore.

If you have selected a location similar to position #5, #6 or #7, as I did, the installation will require a bit more effort but will result in a more integrated appearance.

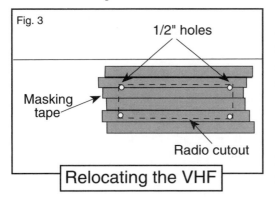

Fig. 3
1/2" holes
Masking tape
Radio cutout
Relocating the VHF

After deciding which of these locations is best for you, place masking tape across the area to be cut out, covering the entire area with a few inches of overlap (Fig. 3). The tape will provide a good surface for marking the area and it will protect the fiberglass from becoming scratched by the footplate on the jigsaw. Using the radio itself or the opening of the flush mount adapter as a template, draw the outline on the tape of the area to be cut. Be very aware of the cabin or lazarette interior; there should be no obstructions or wiring directly behind the area to be removed.

Begin by drilling a ½" hole in each corner of the cutout. This will provide easy access for the blade on the jigsaw. These holes should be placed so they just touch, on two sides, the outline drawn on the tape. Insert the jigsaw blade into one of the holes and, at a low speed setting, begin following the outline and cutting the hole. Use a low speed to avoid melting the edges of the fiberglass and move along slowly so as to create as straight a line as possible.

After cutting out the entire opening, it may be necessary to use a file to smooth off a sharp point or two where the sawn line has met the hole in a corner. With practice, this step will likely become unnecessary.

The next step is to locate and drill the holes required by the frame of the flush mount adapter. Typically, you will need #8 machine screws with a washer and nut. Self-tapping fasteners also work well. In any case, place the adapter in the opening, mark the holes and drill them. The final assembly involves bolting the radio to the adapter, then fastening the adapter to the fiberglass. Be certain to use a sealant or adhesive/sealant beneath the

TIP:

It is not a certainty that a compass adjustment will be needed, but it would be prudent to check for deviation changes.

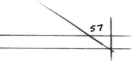

flush mount adapter; 3M 5200 or Boatlife Life-Seal are good choices. Fasten the screws, and the hardware installation is complete. *Note: A faceplate or cover (Fig. 4) is recommended if the radio has an LCD display; in fact, many manufacturers have covers available as an accessory. Continuous exposure to UV will eventually destroy this type of display. If no cover is available and the radio will be placed in an exposed area, it may be necessary to create a cover from teak or acrylic.*

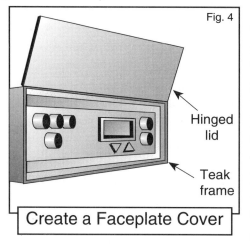

Fig. 4

Hinged lid

Teak frame

Create a Faceplate Cover

Part two of this project involves the wiring. Odds are that the existing antenna cable and electrical wiring will not be long enough to reach the new location. To increase the length of the antenna cable, use prepared lengths of cable which have been fitted with one male end and one female end. These are usually 10 or 20 feet in length, but the issue here is to be certain not to have much cable to spare. If the cable is shielded, it can be almost any overall length, but when the final connection is made to the radio, there should be no more than a few feet of extra cable. If excess antenna cable is coiled, radio reception and transmission will be adversely affected. *Note: In rare instances, it may be necessary to have an electronics supplier create a custom length of cable.*

When extending electrical wiring (and this project has a two-conductor wire that will need to be lengthened), it is always a good idea to match the color of the existing wiring in order to make troubleshooting easier. Regardless of the wire size originally used to connect the radio to the DC panel, it is also a good idea to use at least a 14 gauge wire for the entire length of extended runs. This will help insure the electrical current carried to the radio will be of sufficient voltage.

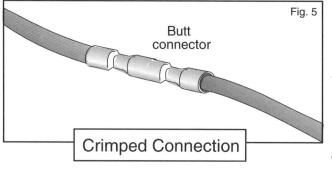

Fig. 5

Butt connector

Crimped Connection

Use a crimping tool to strip the wire ends to avoid breaking off any of the strands of wire within the insulated jacket. *Note: The common practice of using a pocket knife will almost always result in bare wire ends that are missing a few strands. This is not serious unless the overall gauge of the wire has been reduced significantly, thus affecting the wire's ability to carry the rated electrical load.*

After stripping the wire ends, create proper butt splices with the same tool that you used to strip the ends. Use the smallest size splice possible, then crimp the connection in two places (Fig. 5). Be certain to align the color of the butt splice tube to the matching notch color on the tool.

For connecting existing wires to longer new wires, butt splices are common. But another alternative that can be trusted is soldering the wires, then sealing the connections with heat shrink tubing or electricians' tape. Of the two, I prefer the heat shrink.

Allow some slack cable to avoid chafe at places where the cable passes through bulkheads, lazarettes or lockers. Be sure to provide some strain relief on the cable, and install padding at any point at which the cable might come in contact with sharp edges.

Well, that's it. You will likely find yourself using the VHF radio a lot more. At the very least, you will be better informed about what is going on around you.

Chapter Eight
Converting to Refrigeration

I have many fond memories of an O'Day 28 that my wife and I used to sail on Lake Ray Hubbard near Dallas, Texas. The boat was a comfortable pocket cruiser that could carry quite a lot of passengers for her size, both on deck and in the cabin. Among the boat's many accommodating features were two iceboxes — a large one in the galley and a smaller one in the cockpit. Between the two, we could provide lots of space for cold provisions for big parties. But it seemed that no matter how well we planned, we always seemed to leave the dock with cold provisions and come back with fare that was not so cold. Has that ever happened to you?

During those days with the O'Day 28, it became a fine strategy to match the quantity of supplies with the appropriate quantity of ice needed to keep it cold. But no matter how hard we tried, it seemed we could never consume food and drink at a rate that matched the speed at which the ice melted. On several occasions, our guests and crew considered solving this problem by simply consuming all of the liquids on board, but that would have likely created a potential law enforcement problem.

When the weekend arrived, I was always anxious to get to the marina and out on the water; stopping for ice on the way grew quickly from a small inconvenience to a big pain. But with typical Texas summertime temperatures of 95 to 100 degrees, plenty of cold drinks and fruits are needed to help insure that a day on the water doesn't end unhappily with headaches, dehydration, and other heat-related maladies.

It has been proven time and again that, for most of us, the degree of enjoyment we get from sailing is in direct proportion to the degree of comfort we can establish for ourselves while afloat. And to a large extent, that comfort depends on lots of cold liquids. Since the deck had been modified for convenience and comfort, it was logical that the cabin should begin to see changes for the same reason. The first major project below became the conversion of the existing galley icebox to a real refrigeration system.

I began investigating various products and found that, other than size, the options could be reduced to a single primary issue: the source, or sources, of power. Some units operated on AC or DC and switched automatically; some worked on DC only, while still others offered engine-driven or battery operation. As you would expect, each type has its supporters and detractors.

But it seemed to me that any boat attached to shorepower most of the time — which

includes virtually every boat in a marina — should have a system that operates primarily on AC with something else as an alternate power source. In this case, the something else chosen was the ship's batteries.

The unit finally selected was an AC/DC model from Norcolder. It was advertised as a conversion that would fit any icebox up to 6 cubic feet and provide an easier installation than most other units. After many years in the computer industry, I had become accustomed to hearing the phrases "easy to install" and "user-friendly"; often what these cliches really meant was that it was "easy" or "friendly" if you had an engineering degree. But in this instance, common sense, patience and careful measuring resulted in a first-class installation that just about any skipper should be capable of accomplishing.

Like similar units from other sources, this system consists of an L-shaped coldplate that covers the inside of two adjoining walls of the icebox. A single copper line that runs from the cold plate quickly splits into two separate lines on its way to a compressor that is self-contained and pre-charged with freon. The only other components are the switch, fasteners and the wiring.

Sound simple? Well, it was. But a substantial amount of time was required to complete the installation due primarily to the need to construct a platform on which to mount the compressor. Since I prefer to work some and play some — after all, relaxation was one of the reasons we bought our boat in the first place — the total time required was a month of half weekends. We worked on the installation in the morning and then sailed in the afternoon; you might complete the job more quickly with more dedicated effort.

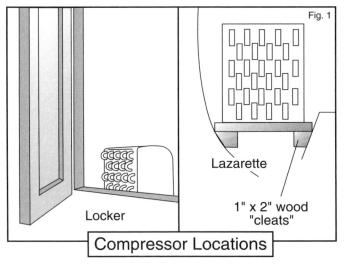

Fig. 1

Lazarette

Locker

1" x 2" wood "cleats"

Compressor Locations

Set aside some planning time prior to beginning the actual work in order to give some thought to the location of the compressor (Fig. 1). This decision will have a greater effect on the success of the installation than any other single factor for three reasons: protection from the environment, noise level in the cabin and air circulation around the unit itself. Other considerations have to do with the typical issues involving any equipment addition to a boat, namely available space, access for service, and its impact on storage areas. Ultimately, a refrigeration system on a boat is very nearly the same as we might have in a home, only smaller.

Protection from the environment is an obvious consideration, as is air circulation around the unit for maximum efficiency. But the most significant consideration regarding the location of the compressor has to do with the resulting noise level in the cabin. In a home, the kitchen is usually at the opposite end of the house from the bedrooms; on board a boat, it is often the same arrangement if your sleeping cabin is the v-berth. But if you have an aft cabin, the compressor is likely to be nearby and, although Norcolder markets a very quiet compressor, when it becomes the loudest sound you hear it can easily be transformed from white noise to a source of sleeplessness.

The bottom line is simply this: Locate the compressor as far as possible from your sleeping cabin, whatever its location. If you have an aft cabin, insulation in the compartment can help reduce the noise level, but airflow around the compressor is required, so a low-level hum will often still remain. There are competitive units on the market that are more costly, and some of these offer a quieter compressor; if you plan to live aboard, the noise level of the equipment may be a more significant deciding factor in the selection process.

On the O'Day 28, the best location I could find was beyond the aft end of the cockpit locker, on the port side, almost all the way to the transom below the steering cables. This locker is a very deep open space with a divider running fore and aft separating it from the "engine room." At the rear of this space, the hull slopes up from the waterline to meet the bottom of the transom.

This location solved several important problems: air flow around the compressor, service room for freon recharging, protection from the environment and, possibly most important, the reduction of noise to the greatest degree possible relative to the sleeping area which, in this case, was the v-berth. There is sufficient copper tubing supplied with the coldplate to allow locating the compressor as far as 12 feet away from the icebox, so the potential choices are fairly broad.

Once the location decision is made, the next major pre-installation issue can be addressed. Almost without exception, a platform of some type will have to be constructed; this provides a level mount on which to bolt down the compressor. We had ample space in the cockpit lazarette for a small platform but, as always, one of the issues aboard is efficient use of space.

To avoid encroaching on storage space already in use in the lazarette, a decision was made to build a platform that would place the compressor astern as far as possible. As it turns out, O'Day provided a substantial amount of empty space located aft below the cockpit sole on the port side. This turned out to be a good choice, and the extra fifty pounds or so placed there had only a small effect on fore-and-aft trim.

In addition to sloping upward, the hull also carried a traditional curve inward at the stern, so the platform (Fig. 2) was shaped to match this, creating a sort of odd-looking triangle — straight across at the front and starboard edges, and curved across the rear. The curved edge also had to be angled downward to match the shape of the hull.

A template of this curved side was made first with poster board, and then with a piece of ¼" scrap wood; the angle of this edge was determined by estimate. After the pattern

was made, the curved rear edge of the platform was cut along with the two straight edges. No adhesive was used to attach the platform to its supports in order to allow for its complete removal should the need arise. The base of the platform was constructed of ½" plywood, to which a sealer was applied.

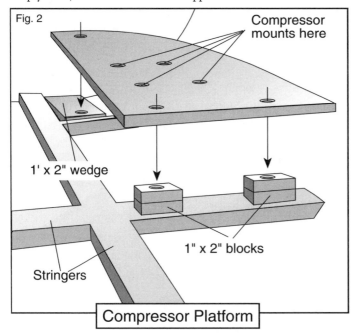

Fig. 2

Compressor mounts here

1' x 2" wedge

1" x 2" blocks

Stringers

Compressor Platform

The compressor is designed to operate even when the boat is heeled, but the recommendation from Norcolder is to mount the unit so it sits level when the boat is not under sail. Since the hull slopes upward towards the stern, the forward edge of the platform required two inches of rise above the stringer that was located at the rear of the storage area. This was accomplished with four pieces of 1" x 2" pine cut to a length of four inches each. These were then stacked two pieces high beneath each of the forward corners in order to achieve the 2-inch rise. As it turned out, this arrangement also provided access to the underside of the platform while installing the compressor.

With the trailing edge of the platform resting on the inside of the hull, support all around was nearly complete. A third piece of wood was cut into a triangle along its longest dimension, and then glued directly to the hull to help anchor the rear edge of the platform. This was located directly aft of the rear-most stringer on the port side.

Once the platform and supports were cut, the entire assembly was temporarily clamped together on the dock so that bolt holes for the compressor and pilot holes for the support screws could be drilled prior to attaching the platform supports to the inside of the hull. A template is supplied by Norcolder that helps to quickly locate and mark the holes for the compressor's mounting bolts.

I use a "Liquid Nails" type of adhesive for most any gluing job that does not involve teak. (For teak, I always use an epoxy.) At the aft end of the locker area is a stringer running athwartships, and it was to the top of this stringer that I glued two sets of stacked 1"x 2" supports that were to be the mounting points for the front edge of the platform. The two pieces of each set were glued together, then the set was glued in place and attached with wood screws. Prior to using the adhesive, the surface of the stringer should be roughened in order to provide a better grip for the adhesive. All glued supports were allowed to cure for forty-eight hours prior to the final installation of the compressor platform. *Note: It is unlikely that any two boats will utilize the same platform shape, size or location. But it is important to recognize that similar pre-installation issues will affect most compressor installations.*

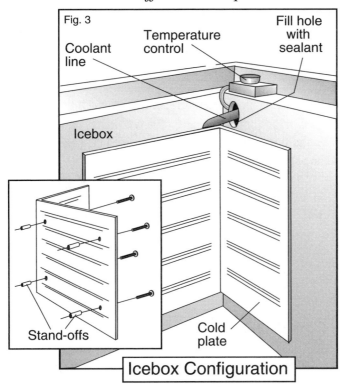

Fig. 3
Coolant line
Temperature control
Fill hole with sealant
Icebox
Stand-offs
Cold plate

Icebox Configuration

The cold plate installation was next. I placed the plate inside the box and marked the location of a large hole to be cut (Fig. 3) that would allow the copper tubing and an electrical cable to exit at the upper rear of the icebox. The copper tubing is only ¼" ID (inside diameter), but the fittings on the ends of each tube are about an inch in diameter. Both of these fittings must pass through this single opening, so the hole must be fairly large. *Note: The coldplate should not be fastened to the inside of the icebox until after the copper tubing has been fed completely through this opening. Unrestricted movement of the cold plate is required to avoid placing kinks in the soft copper tubing while leading the tubing through the bulkhead.*

When cutting this hole, it is important to remember that the opening must extend unobstructed from the inside of the icebox and completely through the bulkhead between the cabin and the cockpit lazarette. This problem is often exacerbated by a sizable air space between the icebox and the cabin/lazarette. Be certain that you will not cut into any wiring that might exist between the icebox and the bulkhead, such as from the battery charger. At the same time, make sure a clean, straight passage is provided for both of the copper fittings. A ¼" pilot hole should be made with an extra long drill bit that extends all the way through the distance required. This will provide a reference for a hole saw that must be used first on the icebox side, and then on the lazarette side. The result should be a straight tunnel for the tubing.

To accommodate the large end fittings, an opening was cut with a 1½" hole saw into

the upper rear corner of the icebox. By bending one of the copper tubes back, I found it possible to push the other all the way through from inside the icebox to the other side of the bulkhead into the port lazarette. With a little effort, the second fitting could then be fed through the same opening. The small electrical wiring harness is fed through last.

The copper tubing is delivered coiled, and must be straightened out in order to make the run to the rear of the locker where the compressor will sit. This must be done very carefully; copper is very pliable, but if a kink is created, the freon flow will be restricted much like a kink in a water hose. The tubing typically has to be curved around hot water heaters or other obstructions just aft of the bulkhead, and the caveat is always the same — smooth, large diameter curves of tubing. The excess tubing must be gently bent into large coils (Fig. 4) no smaller than approximately 18" across, with the fittings pointed down for the final connection to the compressor ports. The two fittings on the ends of the copper tubing are different from each other — one is male and the other is female — so it is impossible to connect them incorrectly.

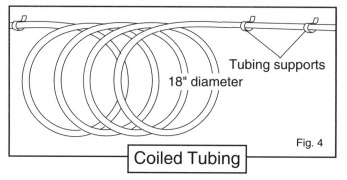

Tubing supports
18" diameter

Fig. 4

Coiled Tubing

The copper tubing will sweat during operation, so it should be wrapped with insulation from one end to the other. For this purpose, an adhesive-backed foam with an aluminum foil cover works well. The last step prior to connecting the tube fittings is to install wiring restraints, nylon zip ties or something similar along the length of the tubing to keep it from rattling.

The adhesive had set on the platform supports, so the platform itself could be fixed in place with 1½" countersunk wood screws in front, and 1" screws at the rear; the appropriate holes had been drilled earlier. Do not glue the platform to its supports; removal of the platform at a later date may be necessary. The compressor is supplied with fasteners and rubber shock mounts that are used to attach it to the platform. Bolt these in place (Fig. 5), connect the end fittings to the compressor with an adjustable wrench, and the hardware portion of the installation is complete at the compressor end.

CAUTION: There are dust caps on the threads of the compressor supply and return fittings, as well as on the copper tubing end fittings. Leave all these caps in place until you are ready to make the final connections. There should be an audible hiss as the locking collars are snugged down. Tighten the fitting beyond this point only about 1 1/4 turns and then stop.

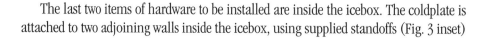

The last two items of hardware to be installed are inside the icebox. The coldplate is attached to two adjoining walls inside the icebox, using supplied standoffs (Fig. 3 inset)

and sheet metal screws. Typically, the walls of an icebox are a soft plastic material better known for its insulating capabilities than for its fastening abilities. Drill holes two sizes smaller than would normally be matched to the screws used on the coldplate, then install the fasteners but do not overtighten. Lastly, a small on/off switch with a temperature control knob is attached to the upper corner of the icebox near the exit hole for the tubing. Once again, don't overtighten the screws holding this in place. The hardware portions are now complete, and it's time to address the electrical wiring.

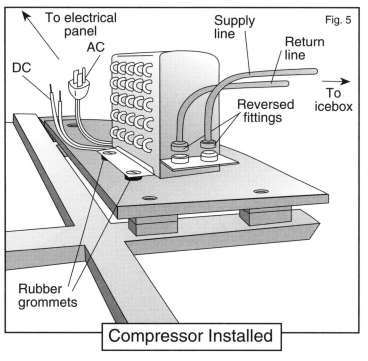

Compressor Installed

This refrigeration unit is designed to work on either AC or DC and, if both are connected, it will favor the AC source. (If one power source or the other is removed, the unit will automatically switch over to the remaining source.) The electrical connections are straightforward, and there are three sections: 1) between the coldplate and the compressor, 2) from the compressor to a DC power source and, 3) from the compressor to an AC power source.

You may choose not to connect the AC portion and, if so, the unit will operate just fine from battery power only. But please recognize that if no connection is made to AC, the ship's batteries are being constantly drained whether at the dock or afloat; a high-amperage battery charger will be required for frequent recharging of the ship's batteries. The availability of shorepower was one of the deciding factors in the selection of this unit, so an AC circuit was planned from the outset.

A pair of wires that connects the icebox to the compressor is comprised of three sections: a short length with a snap connector leading from the on/off switch, a short length with a similar connector leading from the compressor, and a long center extension with connectors at both ends. The center extension has connectors that can only be used in one way, so the ends of the extension are snapped in place between the short wire set at the icebox and the other set at the compressor to complete this portion of the wiring with very little fuss.

At the compressor there is a short three-prong 110-volt cord that can be plugged directly into AC power, as well as a two-wire pigtail that is used to connect the compressor to the DC side of the electrical panel. Assuming that you intend to use an AC power source, a 12-gauge extension of an appropriate length would complete the run back to the main panel where it could be hard-wired directly into the AC side. As an alternative, an AC outlet could be installed in the lazarette, after which the attached cord could then simply be plugged in. My system was hard-wired into the primary AC breaker; the compressor will turn on anytime the shorepower is connected.

Regardless of the method you choose, be certain to tape the connection between the AC cord from the compressor and the AC extension cord that must be added. *Note: Another variation of the AC section installation to the main panel involves removing the plug from the cord attached to the compressor, and then soldering on a length of cord to span the final distance. Once again, be certain to use 12-gauge or heavier wire.*

The DC pigtail must be extended (in this case by adding ten feet) with 12-gauge wire that has been twisted together and led to the main electrical panel. A separate 20 Amp breaker should be installed exclusively for the refrigeration compressor. It's also a good idea to install cable retainers to provide strain relief for the wiring to the panel from the compressor.

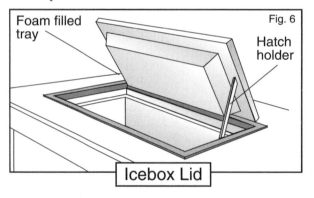

Fig. 6

Foam filled tray

Hatch holder

Icebox Lid

After testing the electrical connections for continuity and ground, the only thing left to do now is turn on the compressor. If the temperature control is set to just beyond the middle, the small ice tray supplied with the system will even make ice!

The final issue to address is that of icebox insulation. In Texas, the difference in temperature between the inside of the icebox and the inside of the cabin can be fairly great. The system will use far more battery power when away from the dock if the insulation surrounding the icebox is not increased. In addition, without added insulation, "sweating" can create a large amount of moisture on the surface of the icebox lid and countertop; if the sweating is too great, the lid will stick in place in the icebox opening due to expansion of the wood trim that usually is present. Often, the only solution is to shut off the refrigeration system and allow the moisture to dry.

So, although it is not necessary, it is highly advisable to cover the outside of the icebox with additional insulation of some type. This can take the form of expandable spray foam, sheets of open or closed cell foam, foil-backed fiberglass sheets or rolls, or almost any type of insulation material. And don't forget the underside of the lid; adding a layer of insulation to the underside of the icebox lid will make an incredible difference in the efficiency of the system. In this installation, the icebox was wrapped with foil-backed fiberglass on the sides and the bottom, and a 3-inch deep plastic tray (Fig. 6) was filled with expanding spray foam and attached to the underside of the lid. Since the foam-filled tray added a substantial amount of weight to the lid, hinges and a spring-type hatch holder were added for convenience.

One final caution: The battery drain caused by the compressor will be relatively great while you are afloat. Be certain to switch to single battery usage when leaving the dock — either "1" or "2" but not "Both" — in order to reserve one battery for starting the engine. Even better, purchase an additional battery and dedicate it exclusively to the refrigeration system, or create a "house bank" made up of two large batteries that are isolated from a smaller "starting" battery (See next chapter.) This can add significantly to the initial cost, but your ultimate satisfaction with the system will be worth it.

Chapter Nine
"I need more power, Scotty!"

How often do you charge your boat's batteries? If you use your boat only on weekends, and leave nothing running during the intervening time, you probably don't have to charge your batteries any more frequently than once a month. On the other end of the spectrum, a liveaboard owner may be required to charge the boat's batteries as often as every other day. But, regardless of the duration or frequency of use, creature comforts and ship's systems must always be balanced against sufficient battery power.

I t is typically the case that, the smaller the boats, the fewer the items that will draw on the available DC current. On a 25 foot sailboat, for example, there will usually be a depth gauge, a knot meter, a fan, a stereo and a VHF radio. On a larger sailboat, say 35 feet in length, you will often add several items to this list: a more powerful stereo, a pressure water system, refrigeration, multiple fans, a GPS, an autopilot and perhaps even an electric flush toilet. It is obvious that the longer the list of amenities, the greater the need for battery power.

Almost universally, a boatbuilder will supply two batteries that can be used singly or together. These batteries are commonly of the commercial variety — physically large in size with the capability of being discharged and recharged hundreds of times. The power of these batteries is designated in either CCA (cold cranking amps) or in Amp hours (Ah) of capacity.

CCA refers to the short-term starting capacity of the battery, which is similar to the way in which automobile batteries are rated; the higher the number, the better. An additional, and perhaps more meaningful, designation is a rating in Amp hours. "Amp hours" refers to the amount of available DC power that can be drained over a period of time.

To determine how long that period of time is, you must add up the ampere rating of all the battery-powered equipment on board, then estimate how long each item will be operated. If, for instance, a stereo requires five amps, and you expect that it will be turned on for six hours out of a twenty-four hour day, then the device will consume thirty Amp hours of power.

A different example could be a radar that is used only intermittently in good weather. While it is operating, a radar could draw twenty Amps. If it is turned on for only ten minutes at a time, six times in a day, then its consumption of electricity is a total of twenty Amp hours (6 uses x 10 minutes per use = 1 hour @ 20 Amps = 20 Amp hours).

The results of all of the consumption calculations for each piece of equipment must

be added together in order to determine how much battery power is required as well as how long all the equipment will operate before the batteries require recharging. And no matter how much battery capacity you may have, it will rarely be as much as you would like. So, what's the solution? Add more batteries, of course! And, as you are no doubt aware, every time we gain something in one place we lose something elsewhere — in this instance, storage space.

Figure 1 illustrates the most common arrangement of batteries. This is a simple system with one battery on each of two "banks" connected by a four-position battery switch that can be set to either "Off," Battery #1, "Both" or Battery #2.

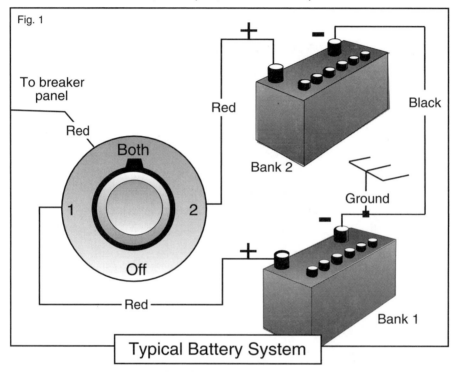

Fig. 1

To breaker panel

Red

Both

1   2

Off

Red

Red

Bank 2

Black

Ground

Bank 1

Typical Battery System

A common practice is to select the "Both" position when starting the engine at the dock, then switching to either battery #1 or battery #2 for ship's power while under way or at anchor. This procedure helps to assure that there will be plenty of reserve power for engine-starting. If both batteries are used for ship's systems, it is likely that there will not be sufficient power to restart the engine. If this occurs, the only solutions are to sail back to the marina and dock the boat, call for a tow, or replace the discharged battery with a fully charged one. Needless to say, any one of these scenarios could ruin your day.

The best solution, however, would be to increase total battery capacity. This can be accomplished on any boat that has enough space to accommodate the physical size of the batteries.

Begin by locating a space that is not only large enough for the additional batteries, but also that provides sufficient access for service. Determine whether or not the batteries will sit fairly level, or if a platform will be needed. If a platform is required, it can

be made from most any wood (Fig. 2). The wood will need to be set in place with an adhesive such as epoxy, or it can be "glassed in," using fiberglass matting and resin. If possible, the platform should be constructed with short vertical sides in addition to a bottom to ensure that the battery will remain in place even in a seaway.

When creating the platform, be certain to allow space for the dimensions of the battery boxes (Fig. 3), and not just the batteries. Battery boxes are not absolutely necessary, but they are a wise precaution against damage should an electrolyte spill occur. In addition to protecting valuables from the battery "acid," the tops of the boxes will cover the electrical connections at the battery posts. To guard against damaging platforms that have been fabricated from wood, be certain to paint the platforms with an exterior enamel or epoxy paint.

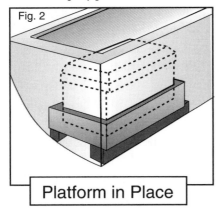

Platform in Place

Speaking of electrical connections... All of the battery cables should (1) be made from "00" size wire, (2) be as short as possible and (3) have connectors on the ends. These connectors should be large enough to accommodate the entire girth of the cable. *Note: It is not good practice to reduce the size of the cable ends in order to use smaller connectors. Smaller connectors will reduce the amount of current supplied by the batteries.*

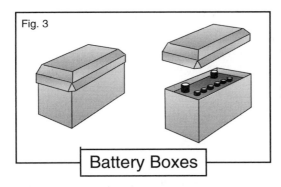

Battery Boxes

After the platform has been built and anchored into place, the batteries and battery boxes can be lowered into the space on the platforms. Then it is time to decide on a location for the battery switch.

The switch can be a duplicate of the four-position switch already in place on the electrical panel or it can be a two-position "On/Off"

switch (Fig. 4). Either way, a switch should be installed so that the expanded battery capacity can be isolated from the original configuration if needed. This switch should be located as close as possible to the extra batteries in order to minimize the length of the additional battery cables. *Note: It is not necessary to install another battery switch, but it is highly recommended.*

Once you have determined the location of the switch, the battery cables can be attached prior to the final installation of the switch. On the reverse side of the switch, you will find three posts clearly marked "1," "2" and "Feeder"; these posts are for the red cables only.

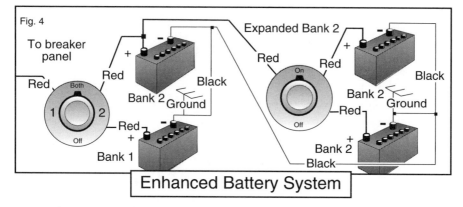

Attach a red cable (of the appropriate length) to each of the new batteries on the posts marked "Positive" and tighten down with wing nuts to hold them in place. Attach the other end of each of these red cables to the posts on the switches marked "1" and "2." A third red cable is then connected to the back of the switch on the post that is marked "Feeder." This "Feeder" cable must be long enough to reach the nearest existing battery. Attach this red "Feeder" cable to the "Positive" post of the nearest existing battery.

Next, connect the two batteries together (Fig. 4) by attaching a black cable to the post marked "Negative" on each battery. On the "Negative" post of the new battery closest to an existing battery, attach a second black cable that is long enough to reach that existing battery. To complete the upgrade, install the battery switch in the location that was previously selected.

Two related issues are worth considering. First, your charger should be at least a 30 Amp system; if not, consider replacing the charger with a unit that has at least this much output. Similarly, if the alternator on your engine is less than 60 Amps or so, you probably should give some thought to replacing it with a high-output version. If you decide to replace the alternator, something in the 100 Amp range, or higher, would make a lot of sense in order to minimize the amount of time required to charge the batteries when away from the dock.

One final thought. Even though you are likely accustomed to charging the batteries with the battery selector switch set to the "Both" or "All" position, it is a good idea to charge each battery bank separately when the number of batteries is not evenly distributed between the two banks. Some DC systems are set up in such a way that this may be impossible. In fact, it may even be the case that both banks will charge only if the battery selector switch is set to the "Both" or "2" position. If this is true for your system, you may have no option but to continue to select the "Both" or "2" position when charging the batteries. The preferred solution, however, would be to rewire the red connections in order to allow each bank to charge separately. This one task may be best left to a professional.

Chapter Ten
Installing a Second Shorepower Inlet

Toys. The word means different things to different people. Ask my granddaughter and she will point to stuffed animals and games. Ask the typical skipper of a sailboat and he or she will point to an autopilot or GPS. Without doubt, the typical boat has more "toys" on board now than in the past.

Many of these electronic marvels operate on 12 volts, and get their power from ship's batteries, which is just fine with me. But most of the big toys still require 110 volts AC and it is the big toys that constitute a potentially longer list — battery charger, water heater, television, air conditioning, toaster, coffee maker, hair dryer. Or how about a VCR, microwave oven or a computer? No doubt the list could be even longer.

Most sailboats are equipped with a single shorepower inlet that provides 30 Amps of service. This is usually sufficient until a device is installed, such as air conditioning, which has a high energy demand. The typical marine air conditioning system will require 20 to 25 Amps of power for normal operation, with an even greater surge demand upon startup.

The problem is that most boatbuilders don't expect us to equip our boats quite so thoroughly and, as a result, we often have to choose which appliances can used simultaneously. Now, there are two possible solutions to this dilemma — be satisfied with the concept of selective use of equipment, or increase the amount of available electricity. For me, it was no contest; I opted for more power.

During our first year living aboard *Lady Greyhawke,* our 1994 Catalina 320, we consistently found that we could use only two of three major AC appliances — water heater, battery charger or microwave oven — while the air conditioning system was running, but not all three at the same time. I suppose this would have been less of an issue had we not been liveaboards, but by the time the beginning of our second year aboard rolled around, we realized something was going to have to change. A second shorepower inlet was the answer.

Power inlets are made in two versions as regards appearance, namely the round stainless steel version and the square plastic type. It makes no practical difference which is chosen; both will likely last for the life of the boat. Our existing inlet is the square plastic version, so that is what we chose as the external hardware.

So far as the wiring is concerned, there are two options here also: (1) create a second circuit complete with AC outlets and a breaker (or two) on the main power distribution panel or (2) create a circuit that is isolated and used exclusively for specific equipment. We chose to install the latter in order to maintain a constant ideal voltage for the air conditioning compressor, resulting in maximum efficiency. In addition, we expected to bring on board one or two more small AC appliances that would add to the existing demand from the main panel.

This project begins with a decision about where to put the new inlet. The location is usually beside, above or below the existing inlet but, in reality, the location could be anywhere on board. In addition to considerations of aesthetics, the location you choose must be free of interior obstructions. There must be sufficient space for a breaker switch and its associated wiring, along with the fact that a sizable hole must be cut.

Once the location has been determined, prepare the area by placing masking tape on the fiberglass where the holes will be drilled (Fig. 1). Masking tape will not only provide an excellent surface on which to mark the centers of the holes, but it will also help to create a cleaner edge while minimizing the mess.

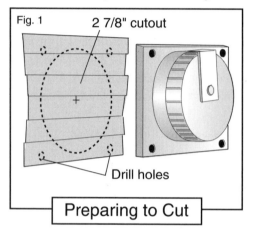

Fig. 1   2 7/8" cutout

Drill holes

Preparing to Cut

In this instance, the new inlet was to be placed to the side of the existing one. A straightedge was used to locate and mark the center of the new inlet so that it aligned on a level with the existing one. You will have to estimate this distance relative to the surrounding area, but be certain to allow at least one inch between the external cases of the two inlets. *Note: Screw holes can also be marked at this time, but it is best to wait until after the hole for the inlet has been cut. Holding the inlet in place within its opening is the most accurate way to mark the holes for fasteners.*

To cut the primary hole, you will need a keyhole saw, a jigsaw or a 2⅞" hole saw that has been fitted to a ⅜" variable speed drill. If the hole is to be cut with a keyhole saw or jigsaw, you will need to use a drill to cut a ½" pilot hole in which a blade can be inserted. This is a tough way to cut this opening, but it can be done.

A faster and easier solution is to use a drill fitted with a hole saw. It is important to note that the drill must be a variable speed model since slow speeds are required when cutting through fiberglass, Lexan and other plastics. If you expect to eventually install other inlets, it might be worthwhile to buy a 2⅞" hole saw, since that is the size required for most manufacturers' inlets. Otherwise, see if you can borrow a hole saw. To cut the hole, hold the drill perpendicular to the surface of the fiberglass, select a slow speed, and apply moderate pressure. If you are patient, the hole will be perfect and the mess will be minimal.

Once the hole has been cut, the inlet can be wired. All 110-volt AC inlets use three wires — white (common), black (hot) and green (ground). This three-conductor wire should be at least 12 gauge (and preferably 10 gauge) in size to safely carry the amount of current supplied. The length of wire needed for wiring the inlet and breaker together is less than a foot, but you may need a total length of up to thirty feet, depending upon the location of the final connection.

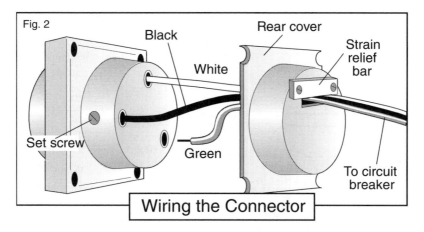

Wiring the Connector

The rear of the inlet has a cover with a built-in strain relief bar (Fig. 2). Remove the screws holding the bar in place and set it aside; the three-conductor wire is then fed through the resultant slot. The rear of the inlet is color-coded to match the color of the insulation on each wire so there should be no possibility of error. Strip about ½" of insulation from the end of each wire, then insert the end into the hole with the matching color. Beside each hole is a setscrew; tighten the setscrew firmly to hold the wire in place. If this step is done correctly, there should be no bare wire visible beyond each color-coded opening. Replace the rear cover, and reinstall the strain relief bar so that the wires are held in place and the cover is snug against the rear of the inlet.

After the wires have been firmly attached, it is now time to install the inlet. Place the inlet against the fiberglass, mark the screw holes and then drill out the holes. Most inlets are installed using #8 sheet metal screws with a length chosen so as not protrude more than ½" beyond the interior surface. Remove the masking tape and you are ready to proceed.

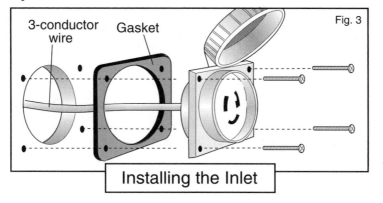

Installing the Inlet

Place the square gasket supplied with the inlet (Fig. 3) between the inlet and the fiberglass surface. A small amount of sealant is placed on both sides of the gasket and the screws are tightened until the gasket just begins to deform. *Note: Overtightening the screws will result in a poorer seal instead of a better one.*

Now it is time to install the main breaker for this circuit. A breaker for this purpose should be 30 Amps with a reverse polarity indicator light just as on the main power distribution panel. The breaker should be installed where it can be readily accessed, and as near the inlet as possible. Select this location before actually wiring the breaker in order to use a length of wire that is as short as possible.

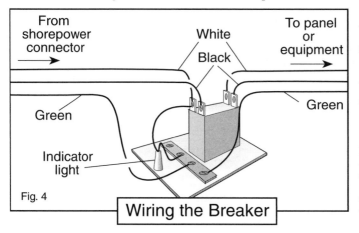

From shorepower connector

White

Black

To panel or equipment

Green

Green

Indicator light

Fig. 4

Wiring the Breaker

The wiring of the breaker is straightforward (Fig. 4), and usually well-illustrated in its accompanying instructions. Essentially, the wires come "in" on one side of the breaker and go "out" on the other side. The length of wire attached to the "exit" side of the breaker depends, once again, upon the location of the final connection. In this installation, the wiring went directly to the air conditioner in the lazarette, bypassing the main distribution panel, so only a ten-foot length of wire was needed.

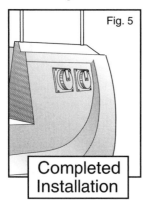

Fig. 5

Completed Installation

Once the breaker wiring is complete, the breaker can be attached to an interior surface near the inlet. As mentioned earlier, the final connection can be made to either the main AC panel, and from there to various devices, or it can be led directly to a specific piece of equipment. In this instance, the wiring was led to a four-outlet AC panel. The air conditioner wiring was rerouted from the primary AC panel and a smaller one located in the aft lazarette, connected to its own 25 Amp breaker switch. This arrangement allowed for further expansion at a later date, if desired. One example of how dual inlets might appear when complete is shown in Figure 5.

Of course, two 30 Amp shorepower cords are required and, optionally, a 50 Amp to double 30 Amp pigtail adapter. This configuration offers a great deal of flexibility when cruising or changing marinas because of the many combinations of electric service that can be derived from a single shorepower connection at the dock.

Chapter Eleven
Adding a Television/Telephone Inlet

If you have owned a boat for any length of time you have no doubt become aware that, when possible, every modification should provide multiple uses. And nowhere is this more true than when cutting holes through the deck or hull. After all, the more openings that exist in the boat's "skin," the greater the number of potential problems.

W hen installing antennas, it is also a good idea to consider a fitting that will provide multiple functions. When installing an inlet for a television antenna, often the best choice is an inlet that is similar in appearance to a shore power connector (Fig. 1).

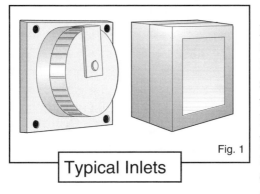

Fig. 1

Typical Inlets

Typically, these inlets are dual purpose with a "coax" TV cable connector sharing space with a marine telephone connector (Fig. 2). It is possible to purchase a TV cable inlet without the telephone connector — but why, you might ask. Even though you may have a cellular telephone now, you may change your mind one day about standard telephone service. Or, too painful to consider, you might sell your boat. Who knows? The next owner might be impressed that the boat was already wired for a telephone.

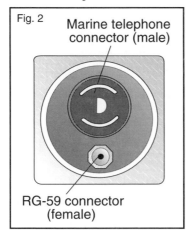

Fig. 2

Marine telephone connector (male)

RG-59 connector (female)

Note: Technically, the coax cable for television, as well as for AM/FM reception, is called "RG-59 75 Ohm coaxial cable." Like all other wiring connections on a boat, this cable should be stranded wire and not solid wire, even at its core. You will likely have to call an electronics supply house to find this cable; retail electronics stores won't stock this type of coax.

At any rate, the cost of a dual function inlet is virtually the same as a single function inlet and, if you never use the telephone portion, you have lost nothing. From a practical perspective, simultaneously running both types of wiring presents little more difficulty than installing a single type. So, for purposes of this discussion, I will assume that you have chosen to install a dual-purpose inlet as well as dual wiring.

To begin, inspect the area surrounding the existing shore power connector in order to determine whether or not there is sufficient space for an additional inlet. It is often most convenient to install all inlets in the same location, but a new inlet could be installed just as easily on the opposite side of the transom or in the cockpit. The keys to a successful installation are ample space for the connector and a logical route for the wiring. Let's install the external hardware first.

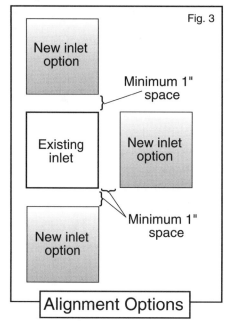

Fig. 3

Alignment Options

Hold the inlet in place at the selected location and verify that it really will fit the space. Using a pencil, mark the outline of the inlet on the fiberglass. If the new inlet is to be placed directly above, below or to the side of an existing inlet, generally align the pencil outline with the center of the existing inlet (Fig. 3).

Set aside the inlet and apply several strips of masking tape to the area that is to be cut (Fig. 4), being certain to overlap the pencil mark by at least two inches in each direction. As in prior projects, the masking tape provides a good surface on which to mark with a pencil as well as helping to maintain a cleaner edge. Measure the distance from the outside edge of the inlet to the center, add at least one inch, and then locate this point on the surface of the tape. This will designate the center of the new hole.

Fig. 4

Masking tape

2 7/8" hole saw

1/2" variable speed drill

Drill

Cutting the Hole

The most commonly available inlet of this type is made by Marinco. Like almost all Marinco inlets, this one will require a hole size of 2 ⅞", and this is done most easily with a ½" variable speed drill and a hole saw (Fig. 4). A ⅜" drill will accomplish the task but you must apply reduced pressure on the hole saw and use a slower speed. If you have no

access to a drill and hole saw, a keyhole saw can be used to cut the opening, but it is unlikely that the result would be as attractive.

Once the hole has been cut, hold the inlet in place in the hole in order to mark the locations of the four holes for fasteners. Typically, these take the form of #8 pan head self-tapping screws of about 1½" in length. Drill these four holes and the drill can be put away. *Note: Machine screws (along with washers and nuts) can also be used, but I have found these fasteners to be no more secure than self-tapping screws.*

The next step is wiring the rear of the connector for telephone service. This is easiest to accomplish if it is done prior to fastening the inlet into place. Most telephone wire will have either a grey or white insulation jacket within which are four wires — red, black, green and yellow. All four of these wires are normally connected during an installation in your home, but for our purposes only the red and green wires are needed. *Note: In the instructions supplied with a Marinco connector, a diagram will illustrate the need to connect the yellow wire also. This can be disregarded.*

Telephone wire can be purchased with an "RJ-11" connector (Fig. 5 inset) at one end and nothing on the other end, or it can be bought as simply a length of wire. If you plan to install a telephone wall outlet such as those found in a house, all you will need is an appropriate length of telephone wire. If you do not plan to install a wall outlet, your final connection will be easier if you purchase a length of wire that is complete with an RJ-11 connector on one end.

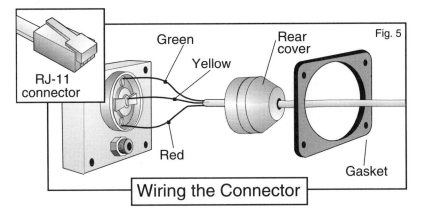

Fig. 5

RJ-11 connector

Green

Yellow

Rear cover

Red

Gasket

Wiring the Connector

Feed one end of the wire through the rear cover of the phone wiring section as well as the gasket that will later be used to install the inlet, leaving about a foot of wire extending from the large open side of the cover (Fig. 5).

As with all wiring, some insulation must be removed in order to expose the bare wire inside. In the case of telephone wire, the strands are very fine, and can be damaged easily if great care is not exercised when the insulation is stripped away. Remove about ½", twist the strands together and then wrap the wire around each of the screw posts. Each post is loosened — but not removed — and then tightened after the wire has been wrapped around it. Figure 5 illustrates where the red and green wires are connected on the rear of the inlet; afterwards, snap the cover into place.

There is nothing unique about the television cable connector; simply screw the coax cable collar onto the male coax post.

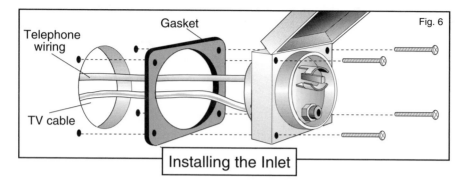

Installing the Inlet

The final installation of the inlet itself is straightforward (Fig. 6). Place a small amount of sealant on the gasket between the gasket and the inlet housing. Press the two together, and remove most of the excess sealant.

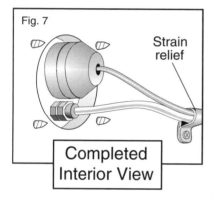

Completed Interior View

Now place a small amount of sealant on the other side of the gasket; insert a screw into any one of the holes in the corners of the housing, and press the complete assembly into place on the boat. Hold the inlet in place while only hand-tightening this fastener. Insert the other three screws and hand-tighten them also, prior to using a screwdriver. Once all four screws are in place, tighten them with a screwdriver and remove any excess sealant. *Note: Silicone could be used as the sealant, but since this is a permanent installation, you would be better advised to use an "adhesive sealant" such as 3M 5200 or Boat-Life's Life-Seal.*

The final step is to install a strain relief cable holder (Fig. 7) near the inlet on the interior side. This will help assure that the wiring connections will remain in place on the inlet when tension is placed on the wiring while pulling it through the boat.

The cable run through the boat will be dependent upon your particular vessel and the location of your television and phone outlet. It should be a route that is as direct as possible, hidden wherever you are able to hide it, and without interfering with storage areas in lazarettes and lockers. Be certain that both types of wire are run together as if they were one, by using two or three nylon tie wraps at the lead end of the wires to hold the two securely together.

After the cable/wire run has been completed, the coax cable can be connected to the television either directly on an RG-59 post or by means of an adapter that will then attach to two screw terminals. Check the reverse side of your TV for specifics.

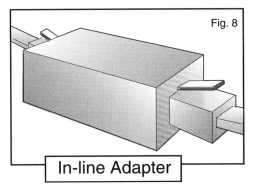

Fig. 8

In-line Adapter

As regards the telephone wire, if you have a cellular phone or no telephone on board, the wire terminus can be almost any convenient hidden location. If you have a standard cord or cordless telephone, the connection can be made with an in-line adapter (Fig. 8), and then hidden. If you install a standard telephone wall outlet, the wiring on the reverse side of the outlet is identical to the wiring on the inlet at the stern of the boat. Choose a likely location, cut out an appropriate size opening, wire the outlet, then fasten the outlet and cover plate into place. The specifics of where this outlet is located will, once again, depend upon your particular boat.

Chapter Twelve
Television Installation and TV Antennas

When sailors talk about electronics, they are usually referring to devices such as a GPS, depth gauge or knot meter. But how many boats have you seen that are also equipped with a stereo, television and video player? Most, I'll wager. And with good reason. The more time we spend aboard, the greater the potential for conflicts between boating and other activities. Perhaps the greatest of these other distractions is television.

Whether you are used to watching weekly programs or pre-recorded movies and events, a TV has become an increasingly accepted part of electronic equipment on board. For this reason, a means of securing a TV or TV/VCR combination is needed in order to avoid damage while under way, along with an antenna of some type. A good solution not only prevents damage, but also allows the TV to be used as conveniently on board as it would be on land. In fact, the best solution results in the ability to get under way without having to be concerned about even stowing the television.

It is often the case that when common conveniences are brought on board, little or no thought is given to what must happen when the boat is made ready for getting under way. It is unfortunate that many boats — especially those of liveaboards — require hours to prepare for even a simple day sail. Although it is quite pleasant to live on a boat, it is even more pleasant to *use* a boat. And, because of this, my suggestions here tend to lean toward those ideas that preserve the option of a sailboat leaving the slip with the least amount of fuss.

When installing a TV, the issues are essentially threefold: hiding the wiring, maintaining an attractive appearance to the area, and devoting the least amount of space possible. On our Catalina 320, we were able to devise a means of satisfying all these requirements and, as a bonus, make the TV disappear when not in use!

The first step is to decide where the TV will be placed. Ideally, it is a spot similar to the concept used in a home, namely that it is visible from all seating but is still in an out-of-the-way location. On a sailboat, this usually means placing the unit on a bookshelf or the top of a hanging locker, building it into a bulkhead or installing a custom platform. All of these ideas work, but some are easier and less expensive to accomplish than others.

On the one extreme, a new boat may have a combination TV/VCR built into the wall of a cabin or a portion of a hanging locker. This is an excellent situation because it addresses all of the issues regarding viewing, appearance and wiring, and does not require special attention before leaving the slip. But on a boat already in use, this solution will likely represent a much larger investment in carpentry than the average owner is willing to spend.

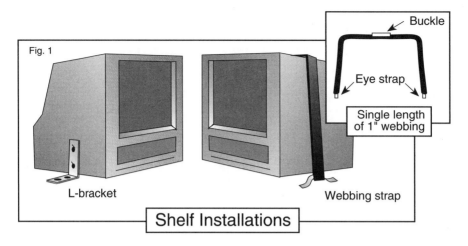

Shelf Installations

On the other end of the spectrum, fastening the TV to the top of a bookshelf or hanging locker can secure it without a lot of fuss. If this is selected as a means of installation, two methods are common: one-inch webbing or stainless L-brackets (Fig.1). If webbing is chosen, the customary method of attachment to the top of the shelf is to use a stainless steel eye strap on each side of the TV, thread a single length of webbing through the eye straps and then fasten it on the top with a plastic buckle.

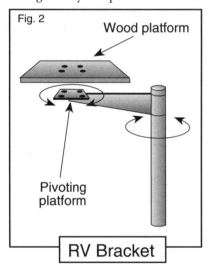

RV Bracket

If L-brackets are used, these should also be stainless and are attached to the sides of the television housing after the internal chassis and components have been removed. Machine screws with fender washers and nuts are used for this step, and it is completed prior to final installation on the shelf. Be certain to unplug the power cord before removing the case, and avoid touching the high-voltage alternating current (HVAC) section after the case has been opened. If you are uneasy about exposing the innards of a television, self-tapping screws may be used to fasten the L-brackets to the sides; however, in a rough sea, this will not be as secure as bolts and nuts. If the case is not removed in order to facilitate bracket installation, exercise extreme care in order to prevent the drill from going too deep into the interior. *Note: If the drill penetrates too far into the interior, components inside could be damaged, resulting in costly repair bills, not to mention the possibility of electric shock to you.*

A third method is to purchase or build a platform that will allow the TV to be installed without using precious shelf or locker space. I have seen examples of this type of installation on many boats, primarily in the form of a swivel platform available from RV shops (Fig. 2). This item, most often used as an auxiliary table in a trailer or motor home, is moderate in cost and attractively finished in epoxy. It is intended for bulkhead mounting, or attachment to any other vertical surface, in order to provide a solid support for the swivel arm that extends about a foot from the mount.

On the end of the horizontal arm is a small plate with holes for four screws where a board can be attached that will ultimately support the TV or other item. The plate on the end of the arm pivots, and the entire assembly can be rotated out of the way and secured easily with shock cord or a strap.

Although the shelftop installation is a good idea, my preference is always for a solution that does not reduce the amount of shelf or locker space; luckily, yet another alternative presented itself, which might find application on newer boats. This solution employs the idea of a swivel platform taken one step further.

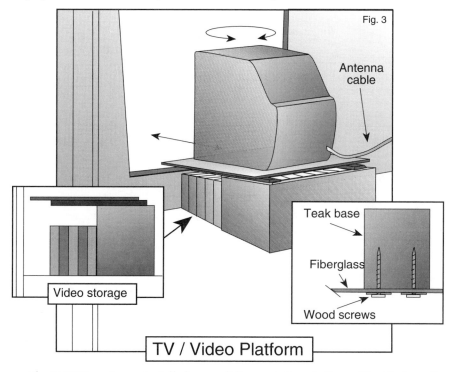

Fig. 3

Antenna cable

Video storage

Teak base

Fiberglass

Wood screws

TV / Video Platform

The TV/VCR unit was installed on a sliding, rotating platform (Fig. 3) that allows the unit to be used, then returned to a hidden position. This platform is often used in "entertainment center" enclosures in a home; doors open to expose the TV, it is pulled out for use, then returned to its original position prior to closing the doors of the enclosure.

To further set the stage, the V-berth on this boat is separated from the main cabin by a door and bulkhead. The bulkhead has two large openings with removable panels that allow for airflow and a feeling of more space. Since the V-berth had already been converted to a cedar closet and large hanging locker, an option presented itself that would not have existed if the V-berth had remained a sleeping area — to create a riser that could support a sliding TV platform. This allows the TV to slide out through the opening in the bulkhead for use, then later be returned to an out-of-the-way position.

To begin this project, a "riser" was constructed that would support the sliding platform at a height sufficient to clear the bottom of the opening in the bulkhead.

The riser was essentially a three-sided box about ten inches tall. It was constructed of ¾" teak that was epoxied and screwed together; then the finished assembly was fastened to the V-berth from beneath with 3" stainless steel sheet metal screws and fender washers (Fig. 3 inset). The platform was then attached to the riser using several one-inch sheet metal screws.

This riser design not only provided a stable base for the platform, but also created an area in which to store video cassettes. The riser itself was finished with a water-based varnish to coordinate with the surrounding trim.

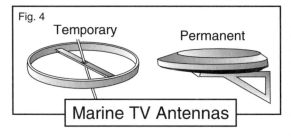

Fig. 4
Temporary
Permanent
Marine TV Antennas

After the installation of the TV platform was complete, the next issue was the antenna. Like most portable TV's, this one had a small antenna attached to the rear, which was inadequate at best. The ideal solution would have included the use of one of the two primary types of omni-directional marine TV antennas (Fig. 4) — either the type that is permanently mounted to a mast or one that is hoisted with a halyard when not under way. Of these, the ideal type is the permanently mounted variety, of course, but it is also the most expensive. These antennas have one thing in common, however: namely that they do not have to be aligned in order to provide the best signal reception.

The permanently mounted type will receive both VHF and UHF broadcasts, while the antenna meant for "temporary" use will receive VHF only. For this installation, an alternative to both of these was devised that addressed reception as well as cost. *Note: For purposes of this discussion, cable systems are not included because cable connections are not available at all marinas, whether foreign or domestic. In addition, cable is not an option on a mooring or at anchor.*

To digress for a moment, VHF broadcasts are received on channels with numbers less than twenty and UHF broadcasts are received on the higher numbered stations. An antenna on a building is designed to receive both types, and the same is true of a marine omni-directional antenna. Since a permanently mounted antenna solution was desired, but the cost was unacceptable, the final solution was to use the existing VHF radio antenna for the lower numbered stations and a loop UHF antenna on the rear of the television for station numbers above twenty.

Even in a house, an antenna attached to the TV is a poor receiver; but on a boat in a slip or at anchor it is even worse. A UHF loop antenna is less affected by movement than a VHF antenna because it does not rely so heavily on line-of-sight for its reception. In addition, although not as ideal a solution as a mast mounted marine TV antenna, the result of this combination has been perfect reception on VHF channels and very good reception on UHF stations.

In order to use the existing VHF radio antenna for TV reception, I needed a switch that would allow the use of one device or the other, but one with a special safeguard. The switch had to include an isolation position so that there was no chance of VHF radio

transmission "bleed-over" into the TV. If this were to occur, the television would likely be damaged in a major way. The proper switch was not found at a marine supplier, but rather in an electronics parts store. As it turns out, the requirement of a switch with an isolation position is a common need in many communications applications.

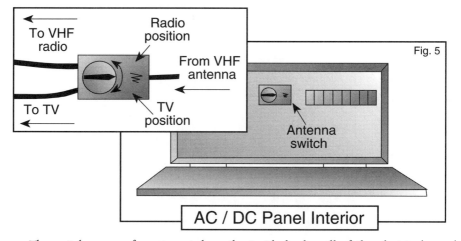

AC / DC Panel Interior

The switch was surface mounted on the inside back wall of the electrical panel cabinet (Fig. 5). The VHF antenna on the mast was connected to the input side of the switch while the two outputs went to the VHF radio and the TV. The television output post required an adapter from the large radio connector to a video cable, which in turn was led to the TV. At the television, I used an adapter to mate the TV cable to a two-wire connector, which in turn was connected with yet another adapter to fit the cable connector on the rear of the TV (Fig. 6). It was to this final adapter that the UHF loop antenna was attached.

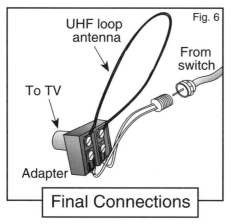

Final Connections

When using this system, you will have to switch between the TV and the VHF radio, but the payoff is a system that works well, is low in cost and is easy to install.

I mentioned earlier that this solution also included "hiding" the TV when it was not in use. To accomplish this, we made simple café-style curtains for the openings in the bulkhead between the V-berth and the main saloon (Fig. 7). These were created with a home sewing machine from a bed sheet in a color and pattern that coordinated with the existing settee upholstery. We also made covers for three small throw pillows from the same bed sheet.

The curtain rods were made from ⅜" wooden dowels, cut to length, found in a hardware store. I fastened the rods in place on one end with a small block of teak, into which a ⅜" hole had been drilled. The other end was inserted into a hole that had been drilled into the hull liner. I fastened the teak blocks to the V-berth side of the

bulkhead with countersunk self-tapping screws, then covered the screw heads using plugs. When finished in a water-based varnish, to coordinate with the surrounding trim, the small teak blocks make an attractive finishing touch.

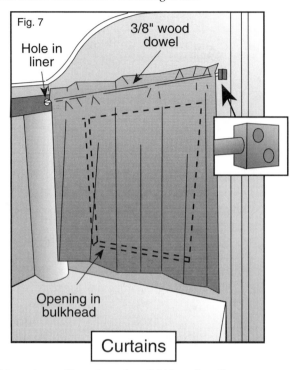

Fig. 7

Hole in liner

3/8" wood dowel

Opening in bulkhead

Curtains

Undertaking this project will produce threefold benefits: 1) a secure, out-of-the-way location for the TV that requires no shelf or loss of storage space, 2) convenient access to video cassette storage, and 3) the retention of an attractive appearance to the interior of the boat.

Chapter Thirteen
Cockpit Speakers and Stereo Systems

To paraphrase an old soft drink commercial, things go better with music. If you have ever spent a day aboard a boat that is not equipped with music in the cockpit, you can appreciate the reason why so many skippers install exterior stereo speakers before almost any other cockpit accessory — after basic instruments, of course.

Just as humidity and temperature affect our mood, so does the presence of music while under way. With the use of automobile audio components, music can be provided to enhance the sailing experience aboard almost any size boat. And with the advent of reasonably priced compact disc changers, an entire day of uninterrupted music is common. Once a stereo with speakers has been installed in the cabin, a set of extension speakers for the cockpit is a natural addition.

The biggest question, as usual, has to do with the best location. These are some of the considerations: Can the speakers be heard well? Are they likely to be kicked? Are they protected from the weather or, better yet, are they waterproof? Will the reverse side of the speaker be unsightly? If so, how will it be covered? Will other equipment, such as the compass, be affected? And so on.

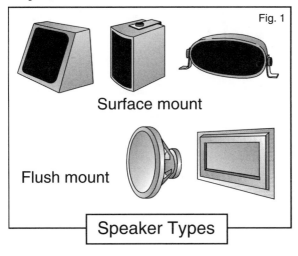

Fig. 1

Surface mount

Flush mount

Speaker Types

Every location in the cockpit will be the best choice for one boat or another. The type of speaker (Fig. 1) will often have as much effect on placement as anything else. A surface-mount speaker, by definition, is attached to the surface of a material in the form of a speaker system within a single enclosure. A flush-mount, possibly also a combination of speakers, is placed into a cutout, and only the grill protrudes beyond the surface. Both types are commonly used on boats.

There are inherent audio differences between surface- and flush-mount speakers, but that discussion is beyond the scope of this chapter. For our purposes, the two are treated as equals regarding sound quality, with the deciding factors being that of placement, personal preference and cockpit design.

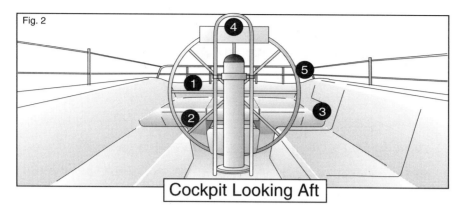

Cockpit Looking Aft

Looking aft from the companionway (Fig. 2), there are several locations that are often used for speaker installation. Positions one through four would require flush-mount speakers, while position five would be useful for small surface-mount speakers; often, two of these locations are chosen. Looking forward from behind the helm (Fig. 3), position six would be a surface-mount, but location seven would require a flush-mount speaker and a cover on the inside of the cabin. *Note: A flush-mount speaker should ideally have at least one cubic foot of space behind it for maximum sound quality. It may be that the enclosure inside the cabin will be too obtrusive to consider this location an option.*

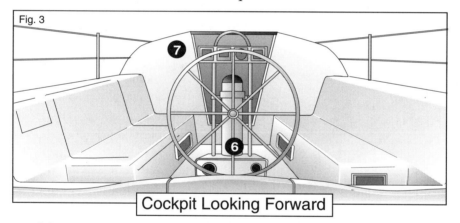

Cockpit Looking Forward

Of these options, only positions four and six are likely to cause a problem with the compass due to the close proximity of magnets on the rear of the speakers. For this reason, speakers are not typically mounted on the pedestal unless the skipper is willing to "swing" the compass in order to make a new deviation card and some adjustments to the compass.

There is an additional location for surface-mount speakers that could apply to many of the newer designs from Hunter and Catalina, among others (Fig. 4). This option calls for installing a speaker upside down beneath each of the stern seats. This location is out of the way, should have no effect on the compass, will provide a wider range of speakers from which to choose and will not require a large cutout. If you happen to own a boat with stern pulpit seats, this may prove to be your best choice.

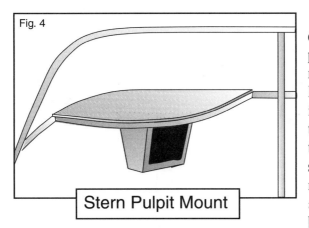

Fig. 4

Stern Pulpit Mount

After the location has been decided, the installation can proceed in a straightforward manner. Be certain to use at least 18 gauge wire (14 gauge is best), and cover all connections with tape or heat shrink tubing. If there is a choice, stranded wire will withstand more chafe than solid wire, and all connections should be soldered. Match the wire runs as closely as possible to existing wiring bundles or harnesses. It is a good idea to surround the wire with silicone or a gasket at all places where chafe might occur, such as the exit through fiberglass or a stainless steel fitting. If surface-mount speakers are installed, try to leave as little wire as possible exposed to the elements.

If rectangular flush-mount speakers are used, prepare the fiberglass surface by using masking tape to cover the area that will be removed. Mark the center of a ½" hole in each corner, then draw the outline of the entire opening. Drill ½" holes in the corners first in order to (1) provide a means by which to insert the blade of a jigsaw when beginning the cut and (2) to allow the blade to turn in the corners once the cut has begun.

If a circular flush-mount speaker is to be installed, prepare the surface with masking tape and use a hole saw of a size that is ¼" larger than the actual speaker. I recommend a variable speed drill that is at least ⅜"; a slow speed and patience work best.

An alternative to a drill and a large hole saw is a jigsaw. If a jigsaw will be used to cut a round opening, mark the outline of the speaker on the masking tape, but plan on cutting a hole that is, once again, about ¼" larger than the speaker. Drill a ½" hole at any point along the outline to provide a beginning and ending point for the blade.

A keyhole saw will also provide a way to create an opening for a speaker. The blades for both a jigsaw and a keyhole saw should be finishing blades with 24 to 32 teeth per inch. Prepare the surface the same as you would for a jigsaw, and take your time. The cutout will require more effort, but the results can be nearly as accurate.

Using silicone or another sealant to prevent water entry into the cutout, apply a small amount of sealant to the entire perimeter of a flush-mount speaker, along with its fasteners.

If your stereo has a fader control, the cabin or cockpit speakers can be easily selected or the two can be balanced for volume. If your stereo has no fader, an inexpensive speaker switch (Fig. 5) can be purchased from an electronics parts store that will provide for the selection of two or three sets of speakers. These devices are typically an on/off arrangement and, except for the more expensive versions, do not offer separate volume controls for each speaker set. Stereo L-pads (volume controls), however, are also available from electronics retailers.

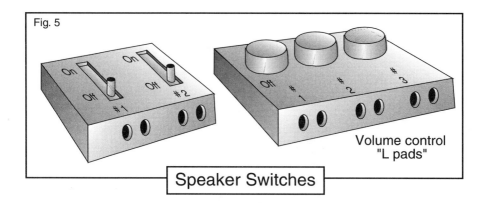

Fig. 5

Volume control "L pads"

Speaker Switches

One final word about speakers — the more you have, the more power you need. If a stereo is rated for 50 watts, that usually means 25 watts per channel. If you have a single set of speakers, 25 watts will drive each one. (A channel is either the left or right speaker). If two sets of speakers are used at the same time, the wattage per channel is divided; in this example, that means only 12½ watts is reaching each speaker. If there are three sets, the power to each one is reduced even further.

Keep in mind that if two sets of speakers are present, but only one set is being used, the power level to each speaker is the same as if both sets were in use. All this is to say that if multiple speakers are in your future, so too may be a more powerful receiver or an accessory amplifier.

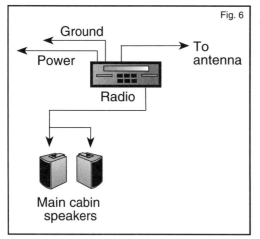

Fig. 6

Ground

Power

To antenna

Radio

Main cabin speakers

If you do not currently have a music system on board, a brief review of options may be in order. Let's start by recognizing that, just like almost everything else for boats, there are "marine" versions of stereo systems. For the most part, these units have gasketed front plates, coated circuit boards and weather-resistant controls. These fine electronics are primarily designed for exposed areas on deck or in the cockpit, and for this application they are well suited.

In truth, almost all installations of audio components are in the main cabin where the equipment is well protected from the weather. For this reason, as well as conservation of space, the vast majority of audio systems on boats are those originally designed for automobiles. And, given the incredible array of options, an audio system on board can produce much of the same sound quality available for our homes. Let's look at some possibilities.

The simplest of systems is comprised of a stereo radio, with integrated cassette or CD player, and one set of speakers (Fig. 6), usually installed in the main cabin. The next step would be to add a second pair of speakers (Fig. 7), in this case designated for the aft cabin. Most all radios provide connections for two sets of speakers, but it is often more convenient to install an in-line volume control, called an "L-pad," between the radio and one or both sets of speakers. *Note: This device must be a STEREO L-pad; there is a significant difference in price and performance between a stereo and a monaural volume control.*

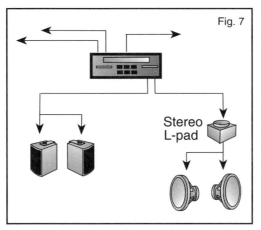

Fig. 7

Stereo
L-pad

On our sailboat, even the speakers in the main cabin are controlled with an L-pad despite the fact that the radio volume control is close at hand. It must be noted that these controls can only reduce the volume — they cannot increase it beyond the setting on the radio; the volume on the radio must be set to what is considered to be the maximum desired.

If your radio is not a high output unit, it may be necessary to add a power amplifier between the radio and one, or both, sets of speakers (Fig. 8). Once again, installing an L-pad to control the volume of each set of speakers may be an option worth considering.

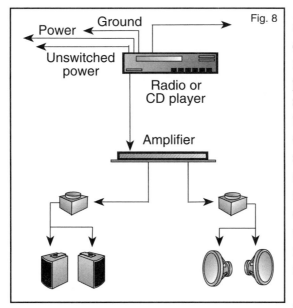

Fig. 8

Ground
Power
Unswitched
power
Radio or
CD player
Amplifier

If you expect your on-board audio system to become significantly more complex than a radio and two sets of speakers, perhaps it would be wise to consider a stereo radio with cassette that also has the capability to operate a CD changer. These systems have become more affordable in recent years, and are even available with remote control. Obviously, more space and money must be devoted to more components, but the results will be worth it.

A decision to invest in a system of the type shown in Figure 9 provides for many options. A third or fourth set of speakers, or more, can be added. If optimum sound quality and output is desired, a power amplifier would be

installed for every two sets of speakers, along with stereo L-pads for each individual set of speakers. Virtually all of these radios provide at least one RCA jack connection for an amplifier, called a "pre-amp output," and many others supply two outputs.

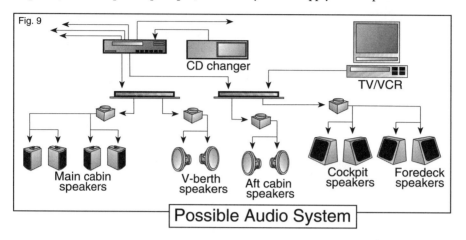

Fig. 9

CD changer

TV/VCR

Main cabin speakers

V-berth speakers

Aft cabin speakers

Cockpit speakers

Foredeck speakers

Possible Audio System

In addition to providing more power for better sound quality, optional amplifiers also provide inputs for other electronics such as a television and video cassette player.

As always, your budget and space aboard are the only limiting factors.

Chapter Fourteen
Bilge Pumps

Did you ever wonder what lies beneath the floorboards in the cabin? Or, daring to venture there, have you ever removed the cabin sole and been surprised to find several inches of water that you didn't expect to see? Have you ever had the pleasure of manually pumping water out of the bilge, only to find that the water had returned a week later? If any of this sounds familiar, it is probably due to a failed pump in the bilge.

T he concept of a bilge pump is a simple idea: a small electric pump that has been wired to a switch and installed near the deepest part of the bilge. A long hose is connected to it that leads to a through-hull where the water can exit the boat. Flip the switch and the pump comes on, emptying the bilge; turn off the switch and the pump stops. Sounds easy enough, doesn't it? Well, it is so long as it actually works.

The tough part is when the pump doesn't come on before the water rises too high or, worse, when the switch is thrown and the pump doesn't come on at all. Both of these problems arise from time to time aboard almost every boat. The solution, of course, is the same solution that prevents almost any problem on board — regular maintenance and/or redundancy.

For most boats, a single electric bilge pump is all that will ever be needed and, almost without exception, a built-in manual pump will also exist. But an electric pump will work only if a switch is thrown that completes a circuit of electricity from the battery, and this is where the problem invariably lies. After some indefinable period of time — usually less than two years — the circuit will likely fail due to corrosion within the wires leading from the pump. At this point, the pump will cease to function. The solution is to remove the corroded part of the wiring, strip the insulation, and then reconnect the remaining wires with appropriate connectors or tape. *Note: After repeated repairs, the pump will eventually have to be replaced if for no other reason than you will have run out of wire to strip and reconnect.*

Will the problem reoccur? Yes, but probably not for a couple more years. Within the preceding scenario, however, there are two issues that directly affect the safety and operation of the vessel: Will you always be lucky enough to check the bilge at just the right time, and will the pump operate when the switch is thrown? So how do you guard against the possibility of potential disaster? The answer is to use a float switch with water-resistant material covering the wiring. Let's look at the wiring first.

Any electrical connection aboard a boat should be protected as well as possible from moisture; it is not difficult to imagine how exposed wires could easily be destroyed by humidity, for example. For this reason, wiring connections must be made that result in

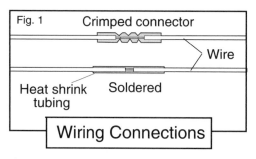

Wiring Connections

a complete cover surrounding the connection. This connection may be heat-soldered or it may be made mechanically with a crimping tool (Fig. 1), and then wrapped with electrical tape, heat-shrink tubing or a liquid "dip" that, when cured, completely seals the wires. As you might imagine, this is even more critical in an area such as the bilge, where measurable amounts of water almost constantly exist.

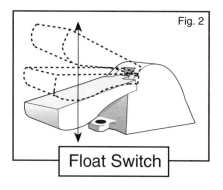

Float Switch

But even after the wiring has been connected and sealed properly, how can you be certain you will arrive in time to turn on the bilge pump before water rises to a point of interior damage? You can't, of course. The best option for preventing water from rising in the bilge, especially for an unattended boat, is the installation of a float switch connected to the bilge pump.

A float switch is a device that is wired between the power source and the bilge pump. The float has a lever on a pivot attached to a housing (Fig. 2), inside of which is located a switch. The lever is typically weighted with an internal metal ball that causes it to orient itself downward. If water rises in the bilge, this lever pivots upward, overcoming the weight inside. When it has risen to near its maximum, the internal end of the lever makes contact with the switch, completing a circuit and turning on the bilge pump. When the water level has been reduced to the predetermined point, the float switch breaks the internal contact and the bilge pump is turned off.

Figure 3 depicts a bilge pump installation in which the pump has been wired to a manual switch on the DC distribution panel; this type of installation relies upon constant

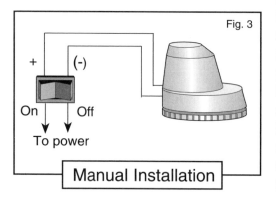

Manual Installation

monitoring in order to avoid a problem. On the other hand, Figure 4 illustrates an installation that includes an automatic switch on the power panel. Whether you are replacing an existing switch or installing a new one, a three-position switch is the best choice, providing fully automatic operation in conjunction with a float switch, in addition to a way to turn on the pump manually.

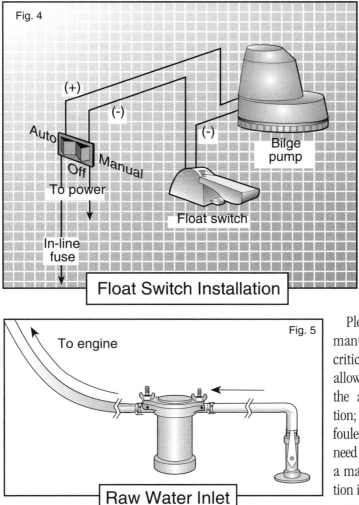

Fig. 4

(+)

(-)

Auto

Off

Manual

(-)

Bilge pump

To power

Float switch

In-line fuse

Float Switch Installation

Fig. 5

To engine

Raw Water Inlet

Please note that a manual position is critical in order to allow for an override of the automatic operation; floats can become fouled and wiring may need to be repaired, so a manual switch position is a low-cost safety measure.

Often, larger boats have more than one bilge pump. Last summer, I came across a 38-foot sailboat that had four bilge pumps, but only two were operational. Consider the consequences if only a single pump had been installed in the bilge!

If you can manage it, two pumps, each with their own float switch, would be an ideal redundancy in almost any boat, but especially beneficial in vessels over 30 feet.

And one last thought — no boat ever sank because of too many working pumps. The ideal combination of a pump and a switch is exactly what you would expect: the largest pump that will fit in the bilge coupled with the best float switch you can afford to buy.

A bilge pump alternative

A second bilge pump could make all of the difference between staying afloat and sinking. This recommendation, of course, assumes that the commonly installed manual pump is also present. But other options exist that don't involve adding to a potentially overloaded DC electrical system. The best non-electrical solution that I have found to

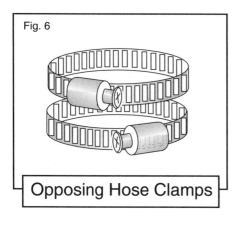

Opposing Hose Clamps

Fig. 6

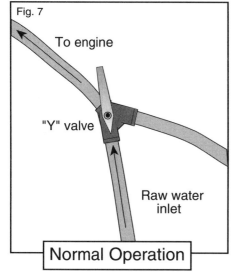

Normal Operation

Fig. 7

To engine

"Y" valve

Raw water inlet

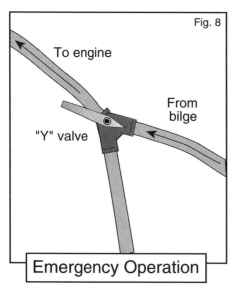

Emergency Operation

Fig. 8

To engine

From bilge

"Y" valve

supplement an existing electrical bilge pump is the use of the engine and its water pump. This system is meant to be used only for emergencies, but there is really only one thing preventing you from using it more often — the supply of water. Let's look at the system's operation.

As illustrated in Figure 5, a wire-reinforced hose typically runs unobstructed from a through-hull valve to a sea strainer to the water inlet connection on the engine. In order to be able to use the water pump on the engine to extract water from the bilge, a "Y" valve must be installed in the hose leading to the engine's water pump. The valve should be located a couple of feet ahead of where the hose connects to the water pump. This hose must be cut, the "Y" valve installed, and then an additional hose attached that will run to the lowest part of the bilge. Each of the hose attachment points should be double clamped with stainless steel hose clamps that have been set in opposition to each other (Fig.6).

For normal operation, the "Y" valve is set to a position that will allow water to flow to the engine from the through-hull (Fig. 7). In an emergency, the "Y" valve is rotated to select the other position in order to permit the engine to operate on water drawn from the bilge (Fig. 8).

There are two things that are critical when removing water from the bilge using the engine's water pump. First — and most important — stop the engine after the bilge has been emptied or switch back to the normal raw water position. As you might imagine, serious damage could result from running the engine for a sustained period of time without water to cool it.

Second, be certain to use a filter on the supply hose leading from the bilge. The engine and its water pump would not take kindly to debris from the bilge floating through the engine's cooling system. This filter could be something as simple as a piece of wire mesh that has been attached to the end of the hose resting in the bilge. *Note: If this type of "filter" is used, be sure to clean it from time to time in order to remove slime or other accumulated coatings.*

Well, that's it. An hour or so of work and the proper supplies can create a simple, reliable emergency bilge pump. Of course, the engine must start, but that's another issue!

Chapter Fifteen
Beneath the Settee

It has been said that you can never be too rich or too thin. When it comes to boats, something else that you can never have too much of is storage space. Most people find that, as they spend more time on board, they develop creative methods of using even the most oddly-shaped spaces. Of all the areas available, the most underused space is invariably beneath the settees.

T he reason for this is quite simple — it is one of the least convenient areas to access. Typically, cushions must be removed, followed by a storage cover board. This wouldn't be so bad if it weren't for the fact that the cushions and covers have to be put somewhere while you are rooting around in the space. And, of course, everything must be put back after whatever is sought has been located. I have lost count of the afternoons during which this process was repeated many times. The solution is to either ignore this valuable storage area or create a convenient means by which to access it; for my part, the latter is the only real solution.

There are two basic approaches to resolving this storage space problem: a door on the vertical face of the settee with a fixed shelf inside, or a door that hides a pull-out shelf or basket. Regardless of the solution you choose, this project is comprised of two parts — the cutout and door on the front of the settee, and the shelf installation. The type of shelf you select will have a direct bearing on what type of door you install, so let's begin with the shelf.

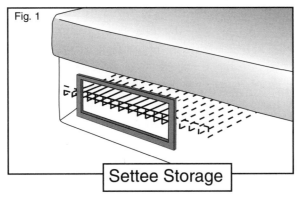

Fig. 1

Settee Storage

The simplest solution is to use a fixed shelf (Fig. 1). This can be vinyl-coated wire, plastic, canvas on a frame or almost anything. The important thing is to provide air circulation, so a solid wood shelf is not a good idea. To affix the shelf to the inside of the settee, short pieces of wood called "cleats" can be fiberglassed or glued to the inside of the hull and interior of the settee. You will need at least two horizontal cleats along the back edge and two vertically beneath the forward edge. The cleats in front should be placed outside the opening of the access door (Fig.2). Virtually any wood can be used for these supports, provided they are coated with a sealer such as varnish or polyurethane; these wood supports are placed where moisture is potentially the greatest.

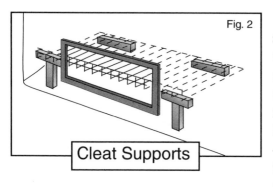

Cleat Supports

Fig. 2

If you would prefer to install a shelf that can be extended beyond the face of the settee for easier access, ready-made solutions are available in most home improvement stores. Once again, an excellent shelf choice is vinyl-coated wire — but this time with a mechanism that provides extension arms and rollers (Fig. 3) similar to supports found in a filing cabinet.

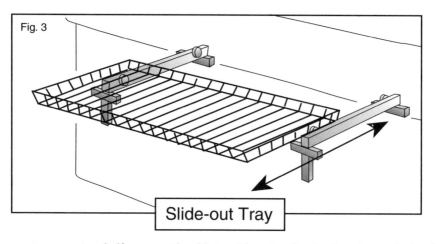

Fig. 3

Slide-out Tray

An extension shelf can provide additional functionality, but has the single drawback of severely limiting the width of the shelf, since it must be able to protrude through the opening of a door. These shelves, as well as ready-made doors, are produced in only a few sizes, so options are limited if movable shelves are your preference. Illustrated in Figure 3 are the same cleats that were used to support a fixed shelf in Figure 2, but in this instance, the cleats are installed in such a way as to support the extension arms.

Regardless of the type of shelf, the installation of a door is the other part of this project. If you have decided to use a movable shelf, it is likely that the size of the shelf has determined the size of the door needed. If the shelf is fixed, the door can be almost any size. Of course, the option always exists to have custom doors made for this project; in an effort to contain cost, however, it would be highly advisable (and far less time consuming) to simply use what is already available. And what is available can be divided into two categories — solid and vented.

Solid doors are available made from plastic, complete with frame, or teak with a frame. You can even use the piece that is removed from the face of the settee when the cutout is made, trim it with wood, and hinge it to a wooden frame. A better choice, however, would be a vented solution such as a louvered teak door, a solid door with openings made by a router, or an enclosure made from mesh and Velcro (Fig. 4).

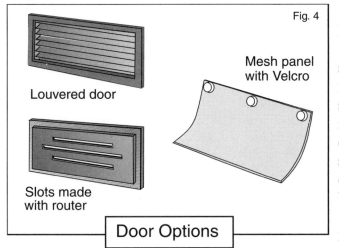

Louvered door

Mesh panel
with Velcro

Slots made
with router

Fig. 4

Door Options

An interesting and highly functional alternative to wire shelves (movable or not) is the concept of a sliding drawer. In its most useful form, the drawer would be stair-stepped to match the contour of the hull beneath the settee (Fig. 5). The opening for this drawer could

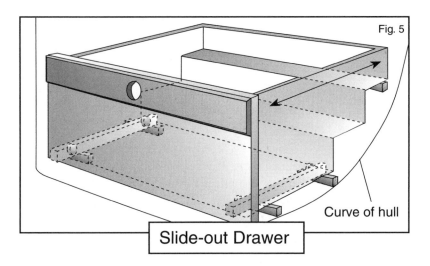

Fig. 5

Curve of hull

Slide-out Drawer

be fitted with a door, but the drawer could also be made in such a way that the door is built onto the front of the drawer. This door could be made to match existing locker doors in other areas, and release with the same type of latching mechanism as other lockers.

But before any shelf and door assembly can be installed, you must first make a cutout that is appropriate to the size of the area available. This cutout is easiest to make with a variable speed jigsaw set to a slow speed. Invariably, people want to complete a project as quickly as possible, but a high-speed setting on a jigsaw can actually slow down the process by causing the fiberglass to melt instead of merely be sawn.

As an aid in cutting and cleanup, place masking tape (Fig. 6) over the area to be

TIP:

It is easiest to mark and drill the holes for fasteners while the masking tape is still in place.

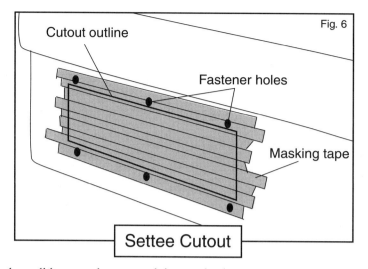

Fig. 6

Cutout outline

Fastener holes

Masking tape

Settee Cutout

removed, draw all lines on the tape and then make the cutout. When you have finished sawing, remove the tape, and with it will come much of the mess.

After the opening has been made, file the rough edges before installing a doorframe or attaching a drawer front. Although not necessary, most frames are installed with a sealant (such as silicone) along with fasteners. The fasteners can be sheet metal screws with finishing washers, exposed pan head screws or countersunk screws with wood plugs. This last option will produce the most attractive final appearance.

If you are installing a door in a frame, it is highly recommended that the hinges be placed on the lower horizontal edge, allowing the door to swing out of the way. It is difficult to move things around in this storage area while holding the door open at the same time. *Note: Although the door could be hinged to one side, the long horizontal format of the door would place a great deal of stress on the hinges.*

To complete the project, a catch of some type will be needed. This item could be a throw bolt, an interior spring catch, a hidden elbow catch (with a finger hole drilled in the door) or one of many other solutions. The primary concern is that the door remain closed even in rough seas.

In some instances, one type of catch is practical for daily use, while a second is employed only while under way. An example is daily use of an elbow catch, with a throw bolt as a more secure backup.

Almost every boat has underused areas beneath the settee and, with storage space at a premium, this simple project can substantially expand your available storage space aboard.

Chapter Sixteen
Polyethylene Shelves

If you have spent much time afloat, you know that little by little the cabin begins to reflect our personal tastes in decorating. Almost before we know it, there seems to be more on board than there is space to stow. The logical thing would be to take some of our possessions home. But is this what most of us do? No! Instead, we search for better ways to stow it, which results in even more room for more of our stuff!

I t is almost impossible to talk about boats without eventually getting around to the topic of where and how gear is stowed. Whether a boat is used for a weekend, a few weeks' cruise or living aboard, virtually everyone agrees that there is never enough locker and shelf space. Areas beneath settees and in lockers can be made more useful by installing vinyl-coated wire shelves or nylon mesh. Both of these options provide not only extra stowage, but also allow airflow for any items placed upon them. But some areas, such as the head and galley, require more specialized solutions.

On traditional boats, these extra shelves usually take the form of nicely made teak products with a pinrail, fiddle or slat across the front and sides. These are handsome to be sure, but they are also somewhat pricey and, most important, available only in a limited range of sizes. Aboard modern boats, materials other than teak are often used to solve storage issues and, among these new materials, are recently developed plastics such as polyethylene.

In the home, polyethylene (poly) and its brethren are typically found in the kitchen as cutting boards, trivets and other food preparation aids. The reason for the emphasis on applications in food handling is the repellent nature of polyethylene's surface; most forms of poly are so slick that mold, mildew and fungus simply cannot get a foothold to grow. On some late-model production boats, this material has been used for various purposes in the head, as well as for binocular and cup holders in the cockpit. Although these uses may seem disparate, they have a single idea in common: low maintenance due to mildew growth prevention and high UV resistance. On our Catalina 320, polyethylene was used rather than teak for fiddles in the head; in fact, there is no teak at all in the head. So, when it came to adding shelves to this area, the most appropriate material seemed to be more of the same stuff that was already there.

In addition to UV protection and mildew resistance, polyethylene has several other properties that make it an excellent choice for a project of this type: it is strong, of medium weight, can be sawn, filed and drilled, and is modest in cost. Although I wouldn't exactly call it lumber, cutting boards made from poly are readily available and can provide the raw stock for many projects of this type. At a local "bed and bath" shop I chose

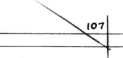

a ½" frosted cutting board for the shelf sections, and a thinner, lighterweight white cutting board for the fiddles.

I planned to make three shelves for the head. The horizontal components were laid out on the ½" frosted cutting board (Fig. 1); the fiddles and mounting pads were cut from the thinner, white cutting board (Fig. 2). The entire project could have been made from a single 16" x 20" cutting board, but I felt the additional thickness of this size board would overbuild the shelves. The fiddles are two inches tall in order to be certain that everything stays put, even in a seaway. The gaps on the front corners between fiddles are intended to facilitate drainage when the shower is used; there is also a runoff space between the wall and the rear edge of the shelf.

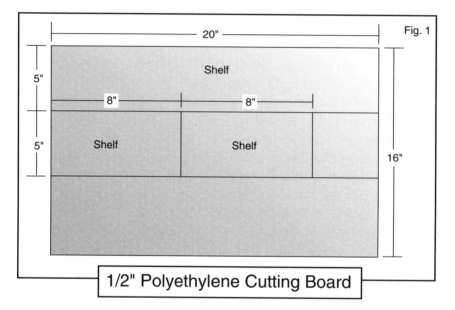

1/2" Polyethylene Cutting Board

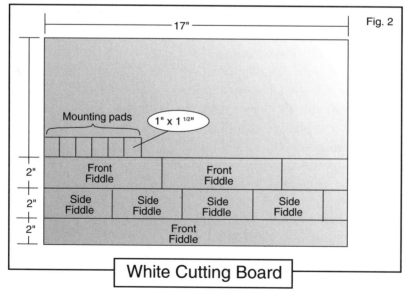

White Cutting Board

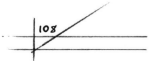

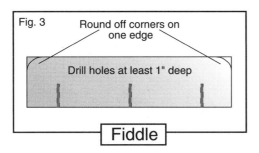

Fig. 3
Round off corners on one edge
Drill holes at least 1" deep
Fiddle

All of the pieces were cut apart with a jigsaw using a blade designed for fiberglass. (A table saw would likely serve better, but it was not at hand.) This type of blade produces a fine edge that requires little finishing so long as the jigsaw is held vertical and a slow speed is used during cutting. On the other hand, polyethylene cutting boards can also be cut with a hand tool such as a keyhole or box saw. If you use a fine-toothed hand saw, very little should be required in the way of edge finishing; this type of saw produces a surprisingly smooth finish. In addition to the jigsaw, I used a Dremel tool with a sanding barrel to round off the front corners (Fig. 3) and smooth the edges after cutting. You will probably agree that it is a real pleasure to work with polyethylene because it can be shaped so easily. *Note: Power sanding polyethylene produces a great deal of fine dust. This is a potential hazard without adequate ventilation, so a mask or other mouth-and-nose covering is recommended.*

After all of the components have been cut and sanded, it is time to drill holes. The shelves and mounting pads are attached to the fiddles using 1½" #6 flathead sheet metal screws, while 1" #8 screws are recommended to fasten the mounting pads to the wall. Drill holes through the shelves from the underside, then countersink all holes. Align the fiddles along the outside edges of the shelves, then set them in approximately ¼" from the edge. Be certain to drill at least two holes into each fiddle from the underside. The side fiddles should be aligned flush with the rear of the shelf. All holes should be drilled into the fiddles at least one inch deep (Fig. 3).

The mounting pads require four holes — two on each side. One set of two will allow the pads to be attached to the rear of the side fiddles using 1½" #6 screws. These holes will be drilled into the vertical rear edge of the fiddles. The other set of two will fasten the mounting pad to the wall, and must be drilled for #8 screws. All of these holes are to be countersunk, but be careful that only two to a side are done in this way. If you have a particularly tight space in which a shelf is desired, the mounting pads can be reduced to about 60% of the specified length. In that case, install the shelf using only one screw per side instead of two. This should not present a problem since a shorter shelf will weigh less and hold fewer items.

Once all of the holes are drilled in the various components, assembly can proceed; use a good silicone or adhesive sealant on all joined surfaces. Begin by attaching the mounting pads to the rear of each side fiddle (Fig. 4) using the sealant and #6 screws. Following this, fasten the side fiddles to the shelves themselves, again using #6 screws and sealant; the front fiddles are the last step.

It is now time to fasten the shelves to the wall. While holding the shelves in place against the wall, carefully mark the four holes on each shelf that will be needed for installation. Drill these holes and, using #8 screws and sealant, fasten the shelves to the wall. The front fiddles were left until last in order to allow room for a screwdriver. If the

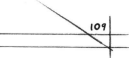

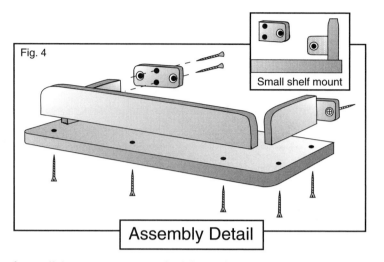

Small shelf mount

Assembly Detail

shelf is of a small dimension, you may find that only two screws are required for the final installation of each shelf unit; the 8-inch shelves presented this option.

The final step is to attach the front fiddles to each shelf. Once again, use #6 screws and sealant, but take care to avoid placing undue stress on the mounting pads. Allow the sealant to cure prior to use. Figure 5 shows how the finished shelves will look.

This project consumed about a day and a half, primarily due to the time required to shape the corners and finish the edges. Because poly had already been used in the head for fiddles, the final appearance was coordinated, if not matched, with the existing trim.

One final note. A relatively new material called "Starboard" has entered the market. It is similar to the material from which cutting boards are made, but it is textured differently and supplied in a thinner raw stock. Handle "Starboard" the same as polyethylene regarding cutting, filing and drilling.

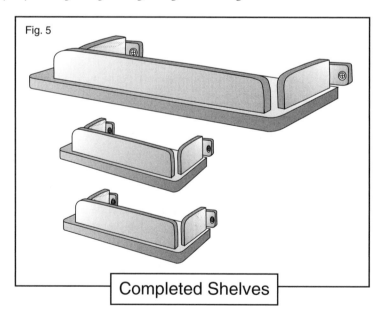

Completed Shelves

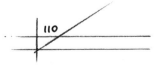

Chapter Seventeen
Galley Upgrades

Whether living aboard or weekending, sooner or later the unavoidable happens — you have to cook something to eat. For a long time, it has been my considered opinion that, when it comes to cooking, if you can't nuke it, it isn't worth eating. The one exception to this perspective is the use of an outdoor grill. Unfortunately, though, many foods don't lend themselves to this method of preparation.

Nonetheless, I have been well fed for many years as a result of a simple agreement with my mate: you cook and I clean. This has proven good for both of us due primarily to the fact that I have yet to meet a cook who enjoys cleaning. But the thing is, no matter what someone is preparing or cleaning, eventually the shortcomings of a galley show themselves.

I am told that food preparation is much easier when foods are easy to retrieve, mess with, and then put away. The same can be said for the clean-up afterwards, and this means that a few modifications are suggested for most galleys.

The drawing below illustrates many of the changes that can be made aboard most vessels in order to provide additional convenience, not to mention increased organization. You may not find all of these changes to be to your liking, but all of them exist

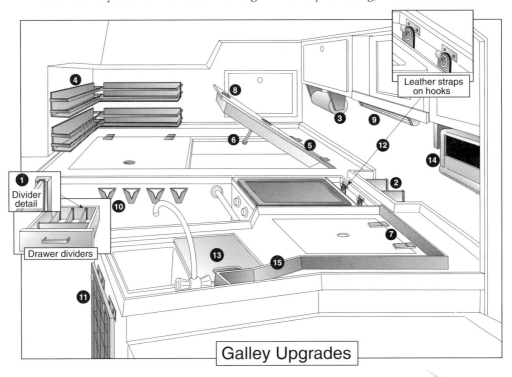

Leather straps on hooks

Divider detail

Drawer dividers

Galley Upgrades

aboard one boat or another in our area, and I have no doubt the same could be said of most any marina in the country. For clarity, the various items have been numbered.

1. To begin, the drawers in the galley can be removed and dividers can be installed. The type of dividers installed here were made from foam core polyethylene using two components — long, flat pieces and end stops (#1 detail). The flats are available in a variety of widths; the material is measured, scored and then snapped cleanly apart. The end stops are adhesive-backed, and are trimmed for height in the same manner as the flats. The end stops are located at intervals, and the flats are then simply slid into place. In the example shown, the drawers were set up for flatware and small utensils. This type of divider won't rust and can be removed, replaced or modified easily. It is also pretty cheap.

2. Since the poly worked so well for the drawers, I also used it behind the stove (#2) in order to organize and store the longer utensils. This was done with a wider size of flat plastic and longer stops, but the method of installation was the same. The only significant difference in this instance was the fact that the end stops were placed along the long dimension instead of at the ends, resulting in a stronger wall between compartments. Depending upon the surface, the adhesive on the end stops doesn't *always* hold, so a temporary sealant such as silicone, 3M 101, Bostick 920 or Boat Life caulk should be used in addition.

3. One of the most popular additions to most galleys is a paper towel holder (#3); almost immediately this item shows its worth. Typically mounted under a locker, this is an easy, inexpensive addition. The only caveat here is to be certain that either (a) short sheet metal screws are used from beneath or (b) countersunk bolts with nuts are installed from inside the locker. Either method will prevent snagging provisions (or your hands), or damaging cookware on the inside of the enclosure.

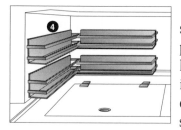

4. After a paper towel holder has been installed, spice racks are often the next upgrade to the galley. If possible, try to make use of the space beneath overhangs or lockers for these items. The option of mounting these racks high near the overhead is attractive if overhangs or under-cabinet spaces have already been spoken for. In any case, these can be "real" spice racks, or a similar alternative often referred to as a "ready rack." The two varieties are about the same size, but the ready rack (shown here) has a more contemporary appearance. "Official" spice racks are often made with pin-rails, which may or may not be appropriate in a modern galley. Once again, be careful of the length of screw that you use for installation, since some of the newer boat designs don't always have as much space between the hull or deck and the liner.

Some boats don't have a bulkhead liner and, for these, a good adhesive may be the only answer. If no fasteners can be used, consider a permanent adhesive such as 3M 5200 or epoxy. The trick to making this work is using acetone to clean both surfaces thoroughly. This preparation will be most important on teak surfaces — the oil in the wood MUST be removed from the surface of the teak in order to have any hope of creating a permanent bond.

5. Except for the smallest boats, virtually all galleys have an icebox or refrigerator with a lift-out cover. The problem is that a place has to be found to put the lid while rummaging around inside the icebox, or to find a third helping hand. To simplify this issue, hinges can be easily installed on one edge of the lid. Two basic choices present themselves — surface hinges (as shown) or a piano hinge with a single continuous hinge running nearly the entire length of one edge.

In considering the choice, remember that a piano hinge is not fastened to the top of the lid. Instead, it is attached to the edge, leaving the countertop less cluttered and smoother. In the project shown here, I selected surface hinges because there was not enough space between the lid and the surrounding opening to accommodate a piano hinge. The same brand and type of hinge already in use was available from a local chandlery, guaranteeing a uniform appearance.

6. In order to maximize the convenience of the newly hinged refrigerator door, I installed a stainless spring hatch holder along the rear edge. This is one of the best hatch holders available for this purpose. *Note: Be certain to mount the hatch holder on an outside edge, or aft, in order to avoid accidentally closing the lid at an inopportune time. An additional hatch holder was also installed on the existing hinged refrigerator door.*

7. In addition to the refrigerator, some galleys also have a dry food storage bin. The lid for this storage area also benefited from the addition of hinges. (For that matter, any lift-out panel can be made into a hinged lid with little effort.) After installing the hinges, I added another spring hatch holder.

8. Often, hinges must be installed in a location not foreseen by the boatbuilder. This means that the existing lifting mechanism may be left unusable due to its location relative to the newly added hinges. Many boats are supplied with a flush-mount lifting ring set into the surface of the lid, while others have a handle attached to the surface. In either case, after adding hinges it may be necessary to also add an additional lifting ring installed on the edge opposite the hinges. Alternately, the existing lifting ring could be moved and the original location refinished.

In either case, if a lifting ring is used, a shallow hole for the large flange area and a smaller, deeper hole for the recessed portion must be made. Take a deep breath: This installation will require some patience, but cutting the hole only a few millimeters at a time will pay off in a finish that looks great.

9. One of the issues addressed in newer boat designs is lighting, but most of the boats I have seen lack sufficient lighting. To remedy this, a DC-operated fluorescent fixture of about twelve inches in length is a good solution. Such a fixture is readily available at most marine retailers, and can be purchased in either single or double tube models. These fluorescent fixtures are wired into the ship's system the same as an incandescent fixture, but will provide more light with less battery drain. Incandescent lighting is softer, more romantic and less harsh, perhaps, but in the galley all this will usually take a back seat to efficient food preparation. *Note: Some of the double-tube fixtures have one red bulb or a red cover for one side; this may be a good choice if night vision preservation is an issue.*

10. Every now and then, a solution to a problem presents itself that is a rare blend of simplicity and low cost. After trying all sorts of things to hold dishtowels and hot pads conveniently, my wife came across a great solution in a housewares store. This little gem is an adhesive-backed plastic triangle with a "V" shaped opening in front. After attaching it to a smooth surface, simply place any corner of the fabric into the "V." We set four of these in a line near the stove; with no additional adhesive needed they have proved to be an excellent solution.

11. No matter how we may try to avoid it, eventually dirty dishes have to be washed, rinsed and set out to dry. But what do you do with the dish rack when it's not in use? Locker storage is too precious. Since almost all dish racks are plastic or wood and can absorb some abuse, they can be placed in a vulnerable location if need be. And so, with this in mind, the solution here was to store the dish rack on a vertical wall near the sink by using stainless steel hooks. These hooks are commonly used with gear hammocks but, due to the deep hook design, they also lend themselves to other purposes. Since the dish rack is held securely out of the way and will remain in place in all but the roughest seas, this placement works well.

Because the hooks worked so well in one place, they were used again in another place — to help store the cutting board that often sits atop the stove. Most stoves are supplied with a cutting board top, but in the instances when this is not the case, suitable matches can typically be found at a housewares store. In either case, the problem is often the same: When the stove is to be used, what can we do with the cutting board? Since there is almost always a space behind a gimbaled stove, an interesting solution presented itself.

12. I installed hooks (#12 detail) behind the stove, along with one-inch-wide strips of leather that were of a length equal to 2 ½ times the width of the cutting board. I set grommets into one end of each strip, while the other end was fastened behind the hook. With the grommet ends hooked in place, a vertical sling was created. When we use the stove, the board can now be removed and placed behind the stove in this sling, still leaving sufficient air space for venting the stove's heat during use. Simple, cheap and functional!

13. A cutting-board top for a stove is typically made from wood. But polyethylene boards are also available and are often used, with minor modification, to serve as covers for galley sinks. In this instance, two were found (only one shown) to be a close match in size to our double stainless sinks. The only effort required was to round off the corners. Whether or not these boards are actually used for food preparation is secondary to the purpose they primarily serve, which is to expand the countertop area.

14. One of the foods I really enjoy is toast, but I object to toasters as well as most other small appliances primarily due to the clutter and counter space required. When I had a land residence, I tried to mount all the kitchen gadgets possible beneath the cabinets, often selecting special models of appliances. On a boat, the underside of a locker is limited real estate for these types of devices, but a compact under-the-cabinet toaster was introduced by Black & Decker recently. With a footprint of about nine by fourteen inches, this is an excellent product for this application. Because it is

horizontal, it operates similarly to a toaster oven, without the need to sit on a countertop. As of this writing, it has been in use about nineteen months, and proves that not everything has to be "marine" to perform well.

15. Almost as common as the desire for additional counter space in the galley is the desire for keeping things *in place* on a countertop. Fiddle rails can help make this possible without the need for tall dividers or complex structures. A marine wood shop was contracted to create a single 8-foot length of fiddle rail, which was then cut into sections to fit the desired shape and location. A saw, a few fasteners and some adhesive are all that you need to add additional fiddle rails to a countertop.

In this case, the fiddle was installed surrounding the dry food storage locker in order to help keep things in place. I extended it to terminate at the faucet for the galley sink, and made a separate fiddle for the other side of the faucet. I used adhesive of the "temporary" type to allow for future removal if necessary. After the angles were calculated and cut, I fastened the ends of the fiddle sections together with screws. *Note: Although you could attach the fiddles to the countertop with metal fasteners, using adhesive alone will hold the fiddles securely while still permitting changes to be made at a later date.*

Well, that's it. Unquestionably, there are additional changes that have been made to the galleys of other boats, and I am certain you will develop yet other ideas. Whether you cook or clean, lots of small changes will no doubt result in an increased convenience in the galley.

Chapter Eighteen
V-berth Cedar Closet

No matter where you live, it seems that there is never enough closet space. The problem of arranging hanging clothes, shoes, coats and folded items is often solved in a land residence by buying an extra dresser, adding another rod to a closet or by boxing up and storing any unused or off-season clothing. But whether you live aboard full time, cruise for a month or stay aboard for long weekends, the issue of where to put clothing — both clean and dirty — becomes an immediate problem on all but the largest of vessels.

Most boats from about twenty-six feet and up will typically have at least one small hanging locker along with some space for folded clothing. If you are the only one on board this may be enough, but it is far more common to find at least two people with stowage needs. And, of course, the longer you plan to be on board, the more space you will need to stow all the stuff brought from home.

It is often the case that limited available space results in a re-evaluation of what is truly needed in the way of personal belongings and clothing. But, just the same, the longer you plan to be on board, the more you will need in the way of clothing out of simple necessity, if not variety. And so it was with my wife, Deborah, and me when we moved aboard permanently. We had to create larger spaces for both hanging and folded clothing, and the most logical location for this modification was the V-berth.

Before we began this project, we looked at other boats and talked to other liveaboards to investigate as many different approaches as possible. What we found were two schools of thought: modify the V-berth if the main sleeping cabin was aft, as we had planned, or press a second head into service. Since we had only one head, we had little choice in the matter.

What we needed most was a long closet rod so the V-berth conversion was based on this requirement first. The area had a shelf forward running across the forepeak, but all else was open and, once the cushions were removed, other options presented themselves. For instance, there was already a lift-up hatch over the starboard locker that begged to be used as a laundry bin. Since the area had no built-ins, long shelves could be installed on one side that would hold the same quantity of folded clothes as would a small dresser. Beneath the shelves would be space for shoes, and the entire area could be lined in cedar panels to prevent mildew, repel bugs and generally keep the area smelling good and the clothing odor-free. We had a plan and it was time to get to work.

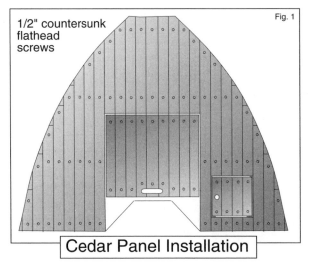

1/2" countersunk flathead screws

Fig. 1

Cedar Panel Installation

The first step was to line the area with cedar (Fig. 1). Originally, cedar panels were to be installed over the curved, vertical sections of the hull (ceilings) as well as across the base of the V-berth, where the cushions used to be. This idea was determined to be undesirable for three reasons: 1) it would cover up the attractive ash ceilings that already existed, 2) the V-berth was large enough so that horizontal panels alone would provide the desired benefits, and 3) we are always cautious about making changes that someone else might not like. This is important when it comes to cosmetic modifications.

To digress for a moment, a change in rigging is likely to be accepted as a permanent improvement by almost anyone coming aboard. The same would likely be true of basic systems upgrades such as refrigeration, electronics and canvas. But cosmetic interior changes are not always viewed in the same light; many potential buyers would find any major interior alteration to be unacceptable if it deviates too far from the norm for that particular boat, especially if it redefines a given space. This realization has come as a result of many interviews with boat owners and brokers.

Now, you may own your current boat for the rest of your life, but if you do, you will be the exception and not the rule. Most people keep their first boat an average of four years, and the next one an average of six. After that, you will find many skippers who will not trade again, but eventually the boat will go into brokerage. If you can undo interior changes, you will be way ahead of the game. Because of this, we modified the V-berth in a way that could be undone and that would return the V-berth to its original use and appearance.

We began by measuring the area of the V-berth's horizontal surface in order to determine the quantity of cedar panels required. These panels are available at most home improvement stores, and are often supplied in boxes containing six four-foot lengths, six two-foot lengths and six one-foot lengths. All stock is four inches wide. For this project, four boxes were required. Happily enough cedar remained after completion to line all the drawers on board. The installation method was straightforward: I used poster board to create a disposable pattern from which two pieces were cut — one each for port and starboard, beginning at the center. The curve of the hull was closely matched as the project proceeded outward from the center. *Note: It is necessary that this project begin at the center in order to create a balanced*

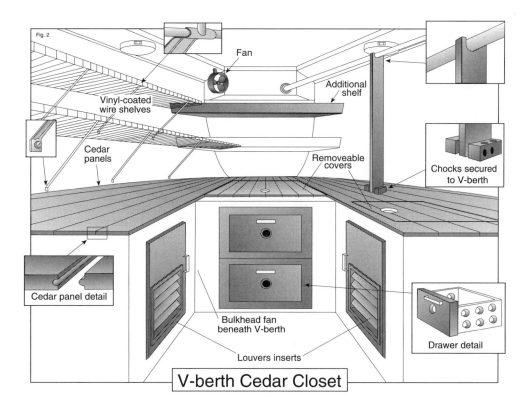

Fig. 2

Fan

Additional shelf

Vinyl-coated wire shelves

Cedar panels

Removeable covers

Chocks secured to V-berth

Cedar panel detail

Bulkhead fan beneath V-berth

Drawer detail

Louvers inserts

V-berth Cedar Closet

visual appearance. In addition, using this method requires you to make the fewest number of patterns.

There are two lift-out covers in the V-berth — one in the center for access to a water tank and forward storage, and a smaller one to starboard above a locker. It is important to mark these covers on the cedar panels so that the cedar can be cut in such a manner as to preserve the lift-out nature of these covers. For this, and for all sawing on this project, I used a jigsaw with a finishing blade for a fine edge. The finger holes in the covers were made with a 1" hole saw after the cut panels were attached to the covers, and the edges of the holes were rounded with a piece of sandpaper.

All of the panels were fastened to the V-berth or lift-out covers, as appropriate, with countersunk #8 screws, but without adhesive. To create a finished appearance, all of the fasteners were arranged in straight lines across the width of the V-berth. The cedar panels are notched along their length by the manufacturer, and this helps to prevent separation of the edges when no adhesive is used. Since there was no adhesive present, the entire installation could be removed at a later date, if desired. The only issue at that time would be carefully patching the holes, and the original V-berth cushions would cover this repair.

The next phase was the installation of a standard closet rod (Fig. 2) on the starboard side. Running fore and aft, it was placed at the maximum height allowed by the space, but not so high as to interfere with hangers being removed and replaced. This was a landlubber's wooden rod of pine, and it required a center support to hold the weight of the clothes. I held the rod in place with typical plastic rod end holders that were fastened to the forepeak and the V-berth bulkhead. I installed the forepeak end using one-inch screws, but through-bolted the bulkhead end and capped it with an acorn nut.

Since a finished appearance is important to me, the vertical support and its chocks were made from teak, then finished with water-based varnish to match the surrounding trim. I cut the support with a 1" hole saw on one end, to form a cradle for the rod, then sanded the entire upper end to round off the edges. The chocks at the base were made from 1" teak stock, and were sawn 2" long to match the width of the support. Ultimately, the chocks were fastened to the lower end of the support as well as through the cedar panels and into the fiberglass beneath.

Next it was time for the shelves. The material selected for these shelves had to offer several benefits: It had to be strong enough to hold the weight, rigid enough to span a length of about six feet, easily removable and — of course — reasonably priced. Most importantly, it had to allow airflow from both the top and bottom of the clothing stacks. This solution was also found in a local home improvement store in the form of vinyl coated wire shelving.

There are several makers of this type of shelving, the most notable of which is Elfa. But since the issue here was shelving only and not a system of storage, I chose a generic brand. If you are not familiar with this material, it is made from vinyl-coated steel; the primary length-wise wire is about ¼", while the wire across the width is perhaps half this thick. One long edge is made with a 1" deep lip that is 90 degrees to the shelf. When installed as designed, this lip is turned downward but, to me, this represented a built-in fiddle so the shelf was actually installed upside down. These vinyl-coated wire shelves are available in a variety of prepared lengths and widths. The size I chose was six feet long and twelve inches deep.

The mounting brackets supplied for these shelves are installed beneath the shelves at a 45-degree angle and fastened to the leading edge of the shelf. In this case, the lower end of the bracket was fastened to the hull liner, using #8 pan head screws and — once again — no adhesive. Four supporting brackets were required for each of two shelves running fore and aft on the port side of the V-berth. The shelves were separated from each other by a measurement of 14" to allow plenty of room for stacking folded clothes. I placed the lower shelf 10" from the base of the V-berth to allow for shoes and other items. *Note: If no hull liner exists, an alternative would be the use of upright supports on the front edge and four 6-inch lengths of 1" wood stock on the rear edge. In this configuration, the wood would have to be glued to the inside surface of the hull since no other anchoring option would exist. Refer to Figure 3.*

Some trimming of the shelves was required in order to fit an odd curve or corner at the ends, and this can be done either with tin snips, a bolt cutter or a hacksaw. I chose the latter because the tool was on hand, and it tends to leave the cleanest edge. Regardless of your choice, I recommend that the cut ends of the wire be coated with a liquid plastic such as rope dip. The wire shelves are supplied with rubber caps on some ends, and these can also be used on the sharp cut ends of wire.

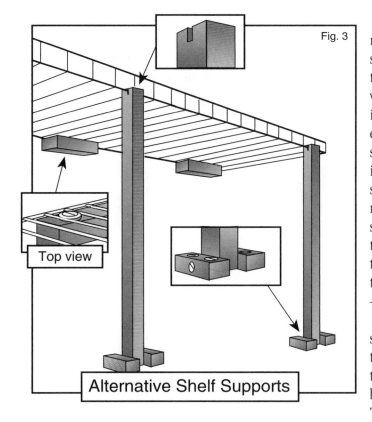

Fig. 3

Top view

Alternative Shelf Supports

Although we now had sufficient storage facilities, the issue of airflow was next. After all, it makes no difference how much storage is available if the items being stowed become mildewed in a short period of time. To address this, we adopted a two-fold approach — vents and fans.

A local wood shop installed rectangular teak-trimmed vents in both locker doors. These vents are ready-made louvered inserts available in a variety of sizes from local chandleries, as well as mail order marine suppliers. We selected vents that were about 4" x 9" in size; after installation, the teak was also finished to match other trim.

For the drawers, we took a different direction. Instead of adding vents that would have been exceptionally small, and therefore of minimal value, we removed the drawers and took them to the same local wood shop to have them modified. In the front, a 1" diameter hole was cut and an off-the-shelf teak trim (finished to match) was epoxied in place. In addition, six 1" holes were cut on each drawer side panel to provide flow-through ventilation.

To complete the airflow phase of this project, we installed two fans, one inside the locker area and one near the top of the V-berth compartment. The internal fan was a 12-volt bulkhead fan made by Nicro — the same one often used in deck vent installations. In this case, not only was maximum airflow desired, but since it was to be installed inside the area beneath the V-berth, the risk of bothersome noise was unlikely. In order to provide complete airflow among all of the areas beneath the V-berth, I cut three 1" holes into the forward bulkhead of the

TIP:

If you can undo interior changes, you will be way ahead of the game.

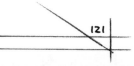

starboard locker, while the fan was installed into the forward locker bulkhead on the port side.

The fan mounted near the top of the compartment was a very quiet, black plastic single-speed fan with a 10-Ohm resistor in line on the power side. This reduction in speed had little effect on airflow, but the noise of the fan motor was lessened just enough to make it "disappear." Although we considered an oscillating fan at first, these tend to be larger and noisier than stationary fans, so we decided against an oscillating fan.

Well, there you have it — twelve running feet of shelf space with six more feet of storage below, along with six feet of half-height closet space. Of course, this is in addition to an existing hanging locker and more drawers aft. For a liveaboard couple, we have found this to be plenty of room for a mix of both seasonal and off-season clothing.

Chapter Nineteen
A Leather Steering Wheel Cover

For many people, handcrafts are a natural extension of other activities, and I am no exception. It has never made much of a difference to me whether the medium was painting, wood carving, casting jewelry, building models, creating dioramas or doing leatherwork. But of the many crafts I have learned, by far the most satisfying has been leatherwork. By working with a master leathercrafter, I learned how to tool designs, carve pictures and create useful, aesthetically pleasing products. Leathercraft offers many attractions, not the least of which is merely the smell of a good hide; often this aroma alone can make the activity a worthwhile experience.

I have made boots, pouches, vests and garment items out of medium-weight leather. From heavy saddle leather I've made belts and carved scenic pictures which were later stained or painted. I even completed a heavily tooled suit of head-to-toe leather armor, based on 15th century patterns, that was regularly used for the protection of the wearer during historic battle recreations. So it was only a matter of time until I began investigating the uses of leather afloat.

Historically, leather has been used for centuries aboard boats as an easily worked, long-lasting material for such utilitarian applications as chafe gear on docklines; liners on yardarms and mast rings; and grips for poles, oars and oarlocks. In addition, decorative uses, such as covers for chests, sheaths for knives, scabbards for swords, and a cover for the ship's log, also have been common.

On board my sailboat, some of these uses have been obvious, while others were not. For instance, the tape that covered the turnbuckles to which the shrouds were connected begged to be replaced with leather, along with matching covers for the chainplates. Our boat has the customary destroyer wheel and stainless steel pedestal guard that we decided could benefit from leather covers. This brought to mind tillers on other boats, as well as boat hooks and downwind poles, all of which would be easier and more comfortable to handle with a leather grip.

The turnbuckles on lifelines, where they latch to the bow pulpit, were another example. And of course, the most obvious application of all, docklines — the eye surrounding a cleat or samson post, the portion that passes through a chock or around a piling, or the many points of chafe along the way from boat to dock. Less obvious decorative uses included the compression post or mast inside the cabin along with the chainstays belowdecks.

As you might expect, a big ingredient in any project of this type is patience. Even though the process is straightforward, you'll likely require more time than you might suspect for each step along the way:

- Measuring the place where the installation will be made
- Creating a rough sketch
- Engineering the design to fit the application
- Test-fitting the pattern
- Laying out, marking and cutting out the various pieces
- Punching all the holes
- Stitching the article together.

With rare exception, a leather item is stitched in place on board, and must be cut apart in order to remove it. This tends to encourage planning, accurate patterns and precise cutting.

Decorative applications often serve a useful purpose, and there is no better place to begin than with the most obvious of all uses — a steering wheel cover. With rare exception, steering wheel covers are made from suede leather. This category of leather has a nap that provides a better grip when wet, and the only care it requires is to be covered when not in use. A leather steering wheel cover can be bought in kit form in limited colors, with or without spoke covers. Or, as an alternative, you can purchase a small suede hide in any of a dozen or more colors, and begin from scratch.

The two dimensions required to create a wheel cover (Fig. 1) are the circumference of the wheel and the circumference of the rim. To begin, measure the diameter of the steering wheel to within $\frac{1}{16}$" from the outside edge of the rim on one side to the outside edge on the other side. This is best accomplished by aligning the measuring device along a set of spokes in order to maintain the straightest line possible. You may remember from high school geometry that to find the circumference of a circle, you use the formula "Pi x D" (Pi multiplied by the diameter). For example, for a steering wheel that is 35" in diameter — not uncommon on many sailboats — the formula would read: "3.14 x 35=109.9" (about 9 $\frac{7}{8}$ feet).

The measurement of the diameter must be as precise as possible; since allowance must be made for other factors, the initial measurement is important. It is impossible to locate a single piece of leather that measures much longer than about four feet, and finer high-end leather skins are often even shorter. In fact, unless the steering wheel is approximately 15" in diameter — the size typically found in an automobile — two or more pieces will have to be assembled in order to create the correct length.

TIP:

Be certain to measure carefully the diameter of your steering wheel to within 1/16".

There are many opportunities to use leather on a boat, with results that produce a little envy and a lot of compliments.

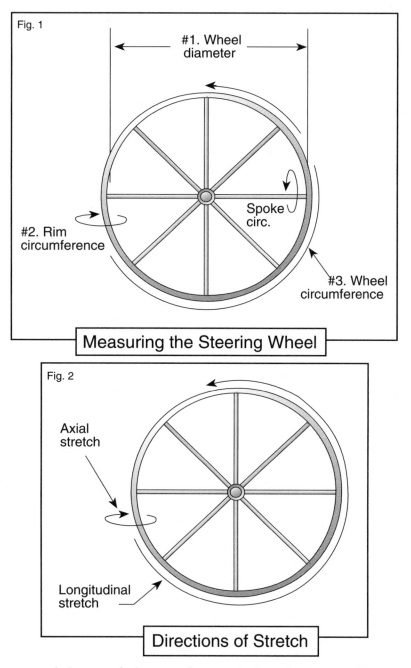

It is a good idea to verify the circumference calculation by also actually measuring the wheel circumference. In lieu of a very long tape measure, this can be readily accomplished by wrapping a string around the outside of the wheel and then measuring the length of the string. Be careful not to pull the string too tight or a false measurement comparison will result.

The second measurement needed is the circumference of the rim. For this, it is often easiest to simply calculate the answer rather than measure the rim; for this steering wheel, the rim circumference was 3 5/16", typical for one-inch stainless steel.

Although creating a leather wheel cover is not quantum physics, there is more to it than taking two measurements, cutting the leather and stitching it on. Before the leather can be cut, the issue of elasticity must be considered and allowed for. The two types of stretch encountered when creating this type of product are longitudinal stretch and axial stretch (Fig. 2).

Longitudinal stretch is the direction along the length of the wheel circumference, and axial stretch is perpendicular to it around the circumference of the rim. Using the example of a 35" diameter wheel, the longitudinal stretch will be about 6%, while the axial stretch will be about 5%. What this means for this particular wheel cover is that the wheel circumference dimension will have to be reduced to 103¼" and the rim circumference dimension will ultimately be 3⅛". When the cover is stitched in place, these calculated reductions will provide for a snug fit that will allow little twist along the rim. *Note: It would be prudent to overcut the sections of the cover and test fit them before trimming to the final length. Verifying the allowance for stretch is important, since some hides will have more or less elasticity.*

As mentioned before, leather is not available in skins that allow for a single piece to be cut to the required size — unless the wheel is as small as those found in automobiles, and even then not always. So the next decision involves where along the rim to place the seams. For a clean look and neat appearance, the best choice for a single seam is usually along the top of the rim at a location that indicates the rudder is straight. For two seams, directly across from one another at the top and bottom usually looks best.

But when three seams are required, which is often the case in larger wheels, style options become an issue. The traditional choice would be to locate one seam along the top of the rim to indicate the rudder position when straight, with the other two at 120 degrees from each other, forming an equilateral triangle. An alternative to this style would be to place the seams at spoke locations — once again at 120 degrees to one another — but without regard for indicating the rudder position. A bit of knotwork or other decoration could then be added to indicate the rudder position. Larger wheels with more seams will require even more planning.

If you decide to use two seams, be extra careful when cutting the leather, making certain that both sections are the same length so that the alignment of the seams on the steering wheel can be nearly perfect. If the alignment is off by much, it will be quite noticeable. *Note: An alternative method of installation is to place a seam at the juncture of each spoke, regardless of the diameter of the wheel. This will require cutting the cover into three, five, six or eight equal pieces. Don't forget to make an allowance in the length of each section for the issue of stretch.*

Once the considerations of seam placement are made and adjustments are applied to the original measurements, you are ready to begin laying out the various pieces that will be required for the cover (Fig. 3). There is always a very specific top and bottom to a hide, so be certain to mark the sections on the *underside* so there is no confusion later about which side is the top. In addition, a more attractive appearance is achieved if the nap of the skin is kept in a single direction; run your hand across the surface and you will easily see the difference. Mark the direction of the nap on the underside as well.

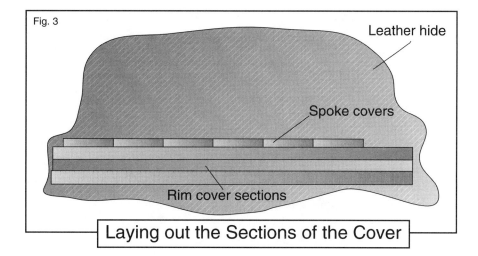

Laying out the Sections of the Cover

Lay out and mark each piece on the underside of the leather. At this time, it would be wise to consider whether you plan on installing full spoke covers, partial spoke covers or no spoke covers at all. It is much easier to lay out and cut all the leather at one time, matching the color shade of the spoke covers with that portion of the wheel to which the spoke cover will be attached. No skin is completely uniform in color across its entire area, so this is a very real consideration.

Many wheel covers are finished with "quarter spokes," spoke covers that extend only 3" to 8" (depending on the wheel diameter) inward from the rim. Some skippers prefer a cover on the "master (rudder) spoke" only; others like full spoke covers, and still others want a combination. In any case, all the parts that are to be cut should be laid out at the same time and the direction of the nap indicated.

Using a utility knife with a new blade, hold the blade against a metal straightedge and draw the knife towards you. Yes, I know: Mom always told you to cut away from yourself, but it just doesn't work here. (I have never been successful cutting leather with anything but a metal straightedge). The idea is to get a clean edge and keep the line straight at the same time. This is best accomplished by making several passes with the knife using moderate pressure instead of one pass that requires effort.

Place the straightedge on the item being cut so that if a slip with the knife should occur, the damage will be to the surrounding leather and not the section you need for the final product.

CAUTION: Since the blade WILL penetrate the leather, cutting whatever is underneath, be certain to place something smooth (and possibly sacrificial) beneath the leather when cutting. This can be a piece of wood, metal, glass or stone. There is a specific product made for this purpose, called a pound pad, that is usually available from the leather supplier.

After all the leather pieces have been cut and the underside marked for both nap direction and spoke placement (if that is the case), the next step is to punch all of the

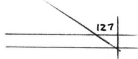

holes required for stitching. For accomplishing this, you have two choices: (1) a rotary hole punch that provides several size options or (2) a single-size small punch with multiple tines. A rotary punch will make holes neither as small nor as numerous, and misalignment of the holes is common.

The other option, a single-size hole punch with multiple tines, is specifically made for this application. It will create either four or eight holes at a time, and is traditionally used with a rawhide mallet. This type of punch results in closely spaced, well-aligned uniform small holes that add considerably to the final appearance of the cover. Single-hole small punches are also available but, like a rotary punch, are difficult to properly align. *Note: If a metal hammer, such as a ballpeen hammer, is used instead of a rawhide mallet some damage to the head of the punch will result.*

Using a hole punch and a mallet (or a rotary punch), punch all of the holes, spacing in from the edge about ¼" and continuing along all of the edges including the ends. Ultimately, the seams connecting the separate pieces will be butt-stitched edge-to-edge to form a complete circle. If you would prefer to have a seam that is turned and stitched in the same manner as fabric, space the holes in from the edge ⅜" on the ends of each section. In order to do this, the thickness of the leather at the ends of the sections must be reduced. A device called a skive is used for this purpose, and then the turned edge is flattened with a mallet or hammer prior to stitching. *Note: Turning the leather under will create a more polished finish but, for most people, it simply isn't worth the extra effort. Unless you are willing to take the time to practice using a skive, I recommend that the ends of the sections be butt-stitched.*

We elected to make spoke covers. Unlike the rim cover, spoke covers are punched only along three sides, leaving blank the end near the hub. Be certain to verify that the marks on the underside of the spoke covers match the appropriate marks on the underside of the rim cover for color matching.

The last thing to do before actually stitching the cover to the wheel is to join together the sections that make up the complete rim cover. These will be stitched together (end-to-end) with a simple whipstitch. The sections should be joined smoothly, with no wrinkling of the leather. *Note: Be certain that the end seams have been drawn together as tightly as possible, preventing the metal underneath from showing through. After an acceptable test fit, the last seam can be closed, and the cover is then ready for installation on the wheel.*

There are two methods for stitching the cover to the wheel — a simple whipstitch or a more time-consuming "baseball stitch" (Fig. 4). The simplest method is a whipstitch, which results in short, straight lines across the edges of the leather, requires a single needle and produces a more rapid completion

TIP:

Remember to test-fit the cover prior to stitching the final seam. The cover should fit snugly but not so tight as to cause undue stress on the seams. If the seams between sections allow the stainless rim beneath to show through, then the entire cover is too tight.

of the project. A more elegant option is the baseball stitch, so-called because it results in a seam that looks like the stitched seams on a baseball — small "V" shapes that connect the edges of the leather together. The baseball stitch requires two needles and half again more time than the whipstitch, but the results are more polished and, to me, much more satisfying. We used the baseball stitch for our wheel cover. *Note: The "baseball" stitch has an additional permutation that results in the appearance of "X's" instead of "V's" across the edges of the leather. As one might expect, this is even more time consuming than the standard baseball stitch.*

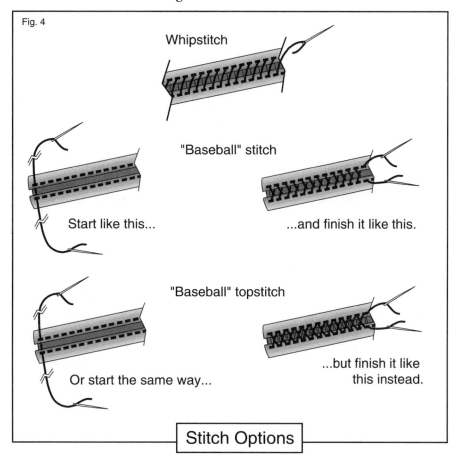

Fig. 4

Whipstitch

"Baseball" stitch

Start like this...   ...and finish it like this.

"Baseball" topstitch

Or start the same way...   ...but finish it like this instead.

Stitch Options

One of the problems common to wheel covers is that they twist on the rim with use, with the result that the seam ends up on the outside of the wheel instead of on the inside of the rim. An easy way to avoid this problem is to use a clear silicone sealant between the underside of the leather and the rim. Apply a very thin coat of sealant a few inches at a time as the cover is stitched closed; when the silicone cures it will create a gasket of sorts. This will prevent the cover from twisting even if a deck ape grabs the wheel.

Using a whipstitch

If you elect to use the whipstitch, begin with a length of waxed thread about fifteen feet long, and knot one end of it. After threading the needle, come through the leather from the underside to the topside, come across to the other side of the seam and push the needle through. Pass the needle down into the first hole, bring the needle through, then back through the original hole and finally out. At the beginning or end of a length of thread — or at a spoke — pass the thread through twice to help reinforce the end of the seam. Bring the two edges of the leather together, and pull the seam closed.

From here, it is on to the next hole from the topside, down and through to the next on the opposite side, through, and then pull the thread tight, closing the seam. This soon becomes a mechanical activity as the needle is drawn down from the topside on one edge, across the seam, through and out the other side, and then snugged up tight. Be certain to pull the thread tight to close the seam after every stitch as you go along in order to produce a consistent and uniform look. Pull the thread just tight enough to close the seam; if the gap will not close, it is undoubtedly because the leather has been miscut. If too much tension is applied to the leather in an attempt to make up for an inaccurate cut, the leather will tear and the appearance of the cover will suffer.

A sailmaker's palm, a metal thimble or a scrap of leather will do nicely to help push the needle through the holes without undue damage to your fingers.

Using a baseball stitch

This stitch requires constant attention and the use of two needles. Begin with a piece of waxed thread that is about twice the length of that used for the whipstitch. With a needle on each end of the waxed thread, bring one needle all the way from the top surface of one side, through the underside of the leather, and through to the top surface of the opposing side. This will result in both needles drawing thread through, from the underside to the topside, but in opposite directions.

Beginning with the left needle, go through the leather from underneath to the next hole on the opposite side of the seam, and draw the needle through. Repeat this stitch with the righthand needle, underneath the next hole opposite; bring the needle through, and then pull the seam snug. Continue this double-needle, double-stitch technique around the length of the entire wheel. When you encounter a spoke, either pass around the spoke — always remembering to stitch to the opposite side — or whipstitch the edge on both sides of the spoke, and then continue as before.

When you encounter the end of the thread, tie it off with a reef knot (a square knot to you landlubbers) and then tuck the loose ends inside the cover on the underside of the rim.

Regardless of which stitch you elect to use, allow four to eight hours to complete the installation of a wheel cover — in addition to the time already spent in laying out, cutting and punching the leather sections. Obviously, the larger the diameter of the wheel, the more time you will require to install the cover. For example, a 30" diameter steering wheel will require about four hours to stitch using a whipstitch, or about six hours using the baseball stitch. By contrast, a 40" wheel cover will take six to seven hours using a whipstitch and eight to ten when using a baseball stitch.

These estimates of time assume that all preparatory work is accurate and that you are reasonably adept with handcrafts. You will find that almost all leather projects will be stitched with one of these two methods, the choice primarily being dictated by the desired final appearance. If you also choose to install spoke covers, allow an additional thirty minutes to one hour apiece, depending upon the length of the spoke. When complete, a leather cover on a wheel that is covered by a wheel bag when not in use will retain its attractive color and texture for many years.

Other applications for leather

The same type of leather that is used for wheel covers can also be used to dress up a stainless steel pedestal guard using the same stitch technique. Suede leather is also often used inside the cabin to dress up a keel-stepped mast, a compression post, chainstays or other chrome supports. Since the interior of a boat provides protection from the elements, the options for colors and types of leather are potentially unlimited. Hides can be of almost any type or texture, providing an opportunity to match colors and interior décor more precisely.

If you choose to make a compression post or in-cabin mast cover, keep in mind that at least two sections will be required to cover the vertical height of the post. You will need to plan the location of this seam in addition to the obvious measurements of height and circumference. A professional way to place the seam would be at the height of a dining table, since a table is usually found near this support. If there is no table or other furniture nearby, place the seam at a height that approximates this height.

Chainstays that match the mast or mast support add a finishing touch that is both elegant and attractive.

Chapter Twenty
Leather Chafe Gear

As pointed out in the previous chapter, leather has historically been used for centuries aboard boats as an easily worked, long-lasting material for such utilitarian applications as chafe gear on docklines, liners on yardarms and mast rings, and grips for poles and oars. In addition, decorative uses such as covers for chests, sheaths for knives, scabbards for swords and covers for the ship's logs were also common. In short, there are many opportunities to use leather on a boat, with the results producing a little envy and many compliments.

The tools used for these projects are the same ones used to produce a leather steering wheel cover — a rawhide mallet, a hole punch, a ruler (preferably with a metal edge), a utility knife, a thimble or sailors' palm and leather sewing needles. The supplies list includes a spool of waxed thread, silicone sealant and, of course, the leather. A sense of spacial relations and a good imagination can help provide a mental picture of the completed project, making it easier to create the pattern.

The type of leather customarily used for unprotected exterior applications is of a variety called oil-tanned, typically available in a medium to medium-heavy weight and most often manufactured in dark brown and black. Its name is derived from a unique tanning process that permeates the entire thickness of the leather with a non-organic oil. Available in skins of about twenty to twenty-five square feet, this type of leather will protect exposed equipment for years, requiring only an occasional application of mineral oil to renew its finish. *Note: It is important that mineral oil, and not an organic oil, be used for the maintenance of oil-tanned leather. If organic oils such as mink oil are applied, the leather will tend to mildew and deteriorate prematurely.*

Although suede leather is beautiful and useful for interior applications or those places that are in some way protected from the weather, oil-tanned leather remains the best choice for exposed applications. It will endure for a relatively long time, maintaining much of its original appearance even years later.

A leather project that does not have a carved, tooled or dyed finish will require little in the way of equipment, and even less in the way of supplies. The primary ingredient, once again, is patience. As mentioned in the last chapter, all phases of the process will require more time than you would suspect. Although an alternative to pattern-making is to contact a mail order vendor who can provide a wide variety of leather items in kit form, the pride of creating something from scratch is undeniable.

Of the many uses of oil-tanned leather, the most universal on any boat, power or sail, is for dockline chafe gear; the bigger the boat, the greater the benefit due to the cost of both the boat and the lines.

For many skippers, boating is not a year-round activity. It may be too hot or too cold; it may be storm season or holiday season. But whatever the reason, it often follows that if boats are given less use they are also given less maintenance, and many boats will sit for long periods of time without attention. With seasonal storms, this can result in belatedly discovering a leak in the cabin, mildew in the head or a chafed-through dockline. With the arrival of early spring, it may be a good idea to consider a close scrutiny of all docklines and the addition to them of chafing gear to help assure a worry-free sailing season.

Typically, adding effective chafe gear to a dockline will increase the useful life of the line indefinitely, the ravages of sun and salt notwithstanding. A good set of chafe gear for a pair of eye-spliced lines will cost about the same as a single dockline replacement, but will last many times longer and provide something the unprotected line cannot — insurance against chafe separation of the line in all but the worst of conditions. Indeed, it has been well documented that effective dockline chafe gear has saved many boats during storms, boats that would have otherwise been lost if not so protected.

In addition to docklines, sailboats present additional applications for chafe gear on turnbuckles, chainplates and the ends of the spreaders. In fact, any place that a fabric or line rubs against a metal fitting is a good candidate for chafe protection. There is nothing more attractive, effective or long-lasting as oil-tanned leather, and it will coordinate with virtually any canvas color scheme or deck/hull color.

For dockline chafe gear to be considered truly effective, it must satisfy three essential conditions:
1. It must surround the entire line as it passes through a chock, over a rub strake or around a cleat.
2. It must resist the environment.
3. It must remain in place.
When properly installed, oil-tanned leather qualifies for high marks on all counts.

On docklines, the most obvious point of chafe is where the line passes through a chock. But on many boats, the deck cleats are set so close to the edge of the deck that no chock is used; here, the cleat itself or the edge of the deck becomes the primary wear point. In marinas with fixed docks, the angle leading from the deck to the dock changes often during the day. The potential for chafe is enough to warrant protection for the line at the dock cleat and the edge of the dock in front of the cleat.

Each of these applications, taken as a single unit, is not a time-consuming project. But since virtually every application is in multiples (two spreader boots or four docklines, for instance), these pieces can collectively require quite a bit of time, usually broken up into small segments.

Most dockline chafe gear designed to pass through chocks will be 10" long, while

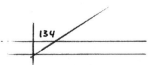

gear destined for a cleat will often be 14" in length or longer. The width of the leather will depend upon the diameter of the line; a ½" diameter line will need a piece of leather that is 1⅝" wide, while a ⅝" dockline will require a measurement of about 2" wide. There is some elasticity in oil-tanned leather, and this is used to advantage when stitching the chafe in place to insure that the gear does not move from the intended position. *Note: It is not unusual to find chafe gear on that portion of line surrounding the cleat as well as the segment passing through a chock; both may be required for complete protection, especially in storm conditions.*

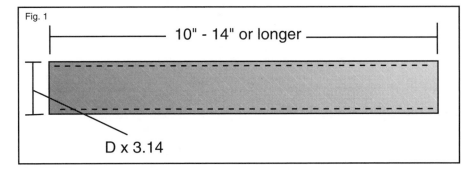

Fig. 1

10" - 14" or longer

D x 3.14

To create dockline chafe gear, identify the line diameter and calculate the circumference using the simple formula referred to in the preceding chapter: "Pi x D" (3.14 x Diameter). Using the product of this equation plus ⅛", lay out the pieces of oil-tanned leather with the proper width for the line in use, along with a long dimension appropriate for the intended application. Using a utility knife and a metal straightedge, carefully cut out the leather, then punch the holes down only the long sides (Fig. 1). Be certain to punch the rows of holes no closer to the edge than ¼" in order to avoid tearing the leather. *Note: Although oil-tanned leather offers a significant amount of stretch, it is relatively easy to tear a punched hole given the degree to which the stitches are tightened. The combination of accurate cutting and controlled thread tension will serve to minimize this possibility.*

To stitch the chafe gear on the line, first position the leather along the inside curve of the line (if it's an eye splice) or opposite from the point of chafe. Bring the two edges of the leather together on the outside of the curve. On at least every third stitch, push the needle through a few strands of the dockline. When complete, this method will result in a chafe guard that will stay in place regardless of weather, wind or wave action. Because the guard cannot be moved once in place, be certain that the guard is precisely where it needs to be when you begin stitching; otherwise it ultimately will be useless. *Note: Moveable sleeves are also useful and are made two to three times larger in diameter than the line circumference. Sleeves are used with anchor rode or in other applications where temporary line protection is desired.*

If you are creating a chafe guard for a spliced eye (Fig. 2), cut a piece of leather roughly equal to the inner circumference of the eye and, by virtue of the fact that the leather has no place to go, it will stay properly in place once stitched around the line. Don't forget to place the seam on the outside of the eye splice.

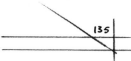

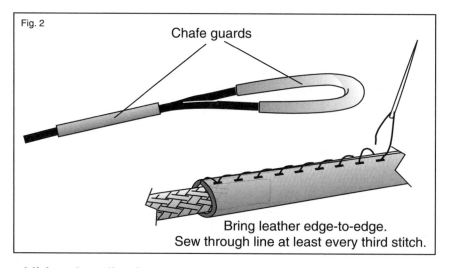

Fig. 2

Chafe guards

Bring leather edge-to-edge.
Sew through line at least every third stitch.

Additional applications

In addition to chafe for rope, sailboats offer two other applications for chafe guards — turnbuckles and chainplates. These deck fittings are most often installed using cotter pins through the ends of the shroud and the pivots on the chainplates. To avoid snagging the headsail during a tack — or for that matter a passing crew member — "rigging tape" is often wrapped around turnbuckles and chainplates to cover the sharp ends of the cotter pins.

As an alternative to tape, PVC pipe with end caps can often be found surrounding turnbuckles and chainplates and, although these solutions are effective, they both lack the one ingredient almost everyone insists upon to one degree or another — beauty. The simple truth is that tape and plastic pipe are unattractive; leather, on the other hand, has long been valued for its appearance, feel and aroma.

Covers for the turnbuckles and chainplates on sailboat standing rigging require more effort, imagination and engineering than dockline chafe gear for three reasons:
1. The covers must be moveable to allow for adjustment of the rigging.
2. They must be tapered on one end in order to fit properly and still be attractive.
3. They must allow airflow inside the cover to prevent mildew growth on the
   leather and rust on the fittings.

The design of turnbuckle covers is more involved than dockline chafe gear because we must lay out a pattern on a flat surface that will result in a shape that is a long cylinder topped by a cone. Consider which of two alternatives you would like to use to allow for moving these covers when rigging adjustments are needed: a cover that slides up and out of the way, or one that is completely removable.

If you would like to be able to remove the cover completely when desired, then consider a polyester zipper sewn into the long dimension of the cover along its entire length. This option allows the cover to be created elsewhere, then simply zipped into place — an attractive option if this is a late-summer or mid-winter project. The zipper needs to be lubricated from time to time, but this design is a popular choice. If you would prefer not to deal with the additional engineering issues that accompany zippers, then your decision will be the same as mine — stitch the item in place and create a cover that is moveable, but not re-moveable.

In either case, the turnbuckle cover pattern begins with measurements of the length and circumference of the turnbuckle. To determine the length of the cover, measure from the top of the turnbuckle downward to a point halfway between the bottom of the turnbuckle and the top of the chainplate, then add 1½" for the creation of the conical top.

The circumference will require more careful measuring since rarely is a turnbuckle circular in shape. (This is not rocket science, but you do need to be as precise as possible.) Typically, turnbuckles are flat on two sides of the long dimension and rounded on two sides; this is important to recognize because it takes more leather to turn a sharp corner than it does to cover a curve. A cloth tape measure will work best for this, but regardless what tool you use for measuring, add about ⅛" to the total for each hard corner turn, usually four altogether. Calculate this new dimension and layout a rectangle that has both the appropriate length and the calculated width. Remember, these covers are to be snug, but moveable.

Now for the tough part — calculating the cutout shapes to produce a conical top. What the top end should look like prior to assembly is three equilateral triangles that have had the top half removed (Fig. 3). There should be three sections of equal width and height spanning one end of the rectangle of leather.

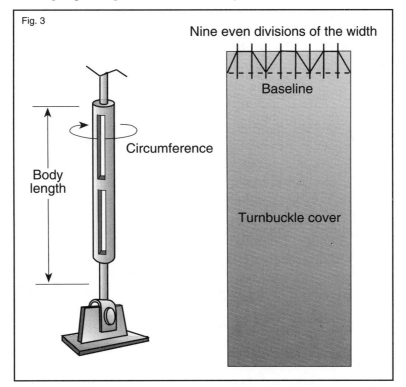

Fig. 3

Nine even divisions of the width

Baseline

Circumference

Body length

Turnbuckle cover

To create these sections, place the underside of the leather face-up, measure 1½" from the end and mark a line (called the baseline) across the entire width. Divide the

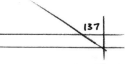

width into nine equal parts, and mark these measurements on the edge of the leather as well as along the baseline. Now draw a diagonal line from the edge of the leather at the baseline to the first mark on the end of the leather, then from the second mark on the end of the leather to the third mark on the baseline. From the third mark on the baseline, draw a diagonal to the fourth mark on the end of the leather; skip to the fifth mark and draw a diagonal down to the sixth mark on the baseline. From the sixth, draw a line to the seventh on the end, and then from the eighth mark on the end to the edge of the leather at the baseline. What you should now see are four inverted triangles — two large ones and two small ones. Cut out the triangles with a utility knife.

The three sections that comprise the cone can be stitched together along the two inner edges prior to the final installation on board. Punch holes along all edges except the ends, remembering to offset the line of holes at least ⅛" from the edge. *Note: If chainplate covers are to be made and attached to the turnbuckle covers, a line of holes will also be needed at the base of the turnbuckle cover.*

Repeat this procedure for each of the turnbuckles on board, typically six to eight pieces in all. It will require about twenty to thirty minutes to stitch each cover in place once the preliminary stitching on the conical top is complete. The final result will be effective covers for turnbuckles that will not only eliminate any possibility of headsail chafe or injury to crew, but will also provide the beauty lacking in other solutions.

Chainplate covers require more engineering than turnbuckle covers due to the rectangle shape presented by most chainplates. However, much of the same procedure is used to make these covers, but with two significant differences: there are four "cone" sections instead of three, and they are of two sizes instead of one.

Determine the height by measuring from the base of the chainplate to a point midway between the top of the chainplate and the bottom of the turnbuckle. For the width, be certain to include any protrusion of the pin in the chainplate, and measure the length at its longest dimension. Once again, allow for the hard corner turns the leather will take, make a note of these final adjustments and cut out a rectangle of leather that has the proper overall size. *Note: Although most chainplates are made from flat steel stock, they are usually thick. Calculate four "hard" corners with an allowance of ¹⁄₁₆" for each.*

Before marking and cutting the conical top section, decide whether or not the chainplate cover is to be stitched to the turnbuckle cover. If so, the finished diameter of the turnbuckle cover must be obtained, since the conical top of the chainplate cover must match the size of the opening at the bottom of the turnbuckle cover. If the two are not to be attached to each other, the diameter of the turnbuckle cover is of no consequence.

As before, place the underside of the leather face up, draw a baseline across one end (Fig. 4), and mark the alternating width and length on the baseline only of the sections of the cone. Okay, now comes the tough part.

Assuming that the chainplate and turnbuckle covers are to be stitched together, calculate the difference between the circumference of the turnbuckle cover and the

overall width of the chainplate cover as it lays flat. Since a chainplate cover is almost always larger in circumference than a turnbuckle cover, this calculation is used to arbitrarily reduce the size of the opening in the conical top on the upper end of the chainplate cover to match the circumference on the bottom of the turnbuckle cover. (Now you know why prepared kits are so popular!)

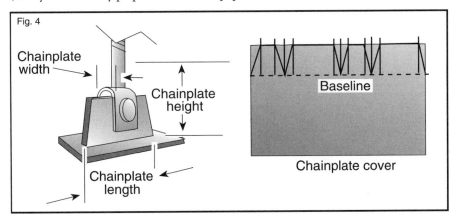

Fig. 4

Chainplate width

Chainplate height

Chainplate length

Baseline

Chainplate cover

Mark the shapes to be cut, remove the excess and punch holes on all edges except the bottom. Stitch the chainplate cover in place as if it were to be used alone, and then attach it to the bottom of the turnbuckle cover. Prior to stitching the chainplate cover to the turnbuckle cover, be careful to align the shape of the chainplate cover with the chainplate itself. For the best appearance, also align the seams of the two covers so that they appear to be one continuous seam.

When complete (Fig. 5), the combination of turnbuckle and chainplate covers will provide unrivaled protection, easy rigging adjustment and aesthetics unmatched by any other solution.

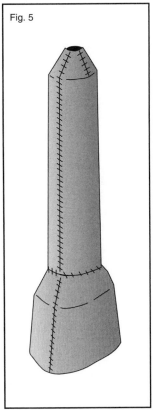

Fig. 5

Chapter Twenty-one
Spit and Polish

When considering improvements aboard our boats, the projects that come to mind most often are such items as additional sail handling gear or canvas, cabinetry, a generator or even sophisticated electronics. But how about considering the appearance of the boat?

The exterior can be enhanced in several ways — adding painted or vinyl graphics, changing the color of the stripes, refinishing the wood, or polishing the smooth fiberglass areas of the deck and hull. Of these possibilities, the least costly option that will improve the appearance of the exterior is a good polish job. Unfortunately, polishing a boat is hot, hard work.

Some skippers neither polish their own boats nor hire this service. The result is a greatly reduced life expectancy of the gelcoat due to oxidation. Oxidation is a chalky powder that is produced when ultraviolet from the sun is allowed to destroy an unprotected gelcoat surface. But the hard shell protection of a layer of regularly renewed wax on the surface of the gelcoat can prevent this oxidation from occurring. The gelcoat provides not only a high gloss, but also ultraviolet protection of the fiberglass beneath. So if the gelcoat is permitted to oxidize completely, no protection remains for the fiberglass.

If you own a new boat, it can remain new-looking indefinitely if it is washed every two weeks and polished at least twice a year. If you own an older boat, this same routine is recommended, provided that at least some gelcoat still exists; the boat won't look *new* but it can look *great*. If the gelcoat is completely oxidized, no manner of polishing will restore the original shine. Polishing will, however, seal the surface of the fiberglass and offer a minimum of protection from the sun's damaging ultraviolet rays. If the gelcoat completely disappears due to oxidation, the only option remaining, other than continued inaction, is to paint the boat.

In an effort to contain maintenance costs, many skippers polish their own boats instead of contracting for this service. And, given proper instruction, tools and supplies, most people should expect to see a satisfying result. The biggest obstacle to a successful polishing job is a psychological one: A boat hull can loom very large when viewed from the perspective of a seat on the dock or a dinghy alongside. A typical 35 footer will seem huge when the bow cannot be seen from a position at the stern. In addition, the deck can appear to be the size of a football field when we are on our hands and knees, crawling across its entire surface.

Truly, this is not a glamorous job. But, if you decide to do this yourself, some assistance will help make the result more professional.

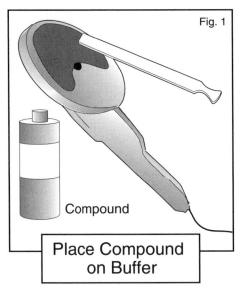

Fig. 1

Compound

Place Compound on Buffer

First, some definitions are in order. *Compound* is a paste that contains an abrasive; it is used to remove oxidation and smooth the surface of the gelcoat. *Wax*, whether paste or liquid, is the stuff that makes the gelcoat shine. *Polishing* is the activity that puts these materials to use, and ultimately results in a gloss surface.

As you might expect, there are several makers of compounds and waxes — 3M, Meguiars and Star-Brite, to name a few. But, regardless of the brand, application is the key and so long as the material inside the bottle is of a marine grade, the results should be good.

Begin the process with a thorough wash of the fiberglass surface. This wash will remove minor stains, pollution and dirt as well as light to moderate amounts of oxidation; the boat must be allowed to dry completely before proceeding with any attempts at polishing the surface. If moderate levels of oxidation were present, an abrasive compound will be required in addition to a wax. Essentially, this means that the boat will polished twice, once to compound and once to wax.

Almost without exception, there will be isolated spots such as docking marks or stains that will need to be removed with compound. In addition, irregularities in the surface shine will require compound in order to eliminate "flat spots" in the gelcoat; wax alone typically will not produce the best results. If only small areas will need to be compounded, the compound material can be used on a rough cloth such as a terrycloth towel. If large areas are to be treated, consider an electric buffer a necessary tool.

After the boat has been washed and allowed to dry, begin the process of compounding by placing a small amount of material on the pad of a heavy duty 8" buffer such as those made by Makita or Porter Cable. This is facilitated by the use of a paint stirring stick (Fig. 1). *Note: A buffer made for automobiles has neither the speed nor the power required for compounding gelcoat.*

If large areas of the hull are stained, an additional step may be required before the compounding can begin. For example, along many stretches of the Intercoastal Waterway, iron deposits (ferrous oxides) in the water can cause a mustard-colored stain to appear on the bows of fiberglass boats. This stain will be difficult to remove with an abrasive compound, but will come away easily with oxalic acid. If rust stains are present from metal through-hulls above the waterline, a product such as FSR (Fiberglass Stain Remover) may be needed. If you are unsure about what might have caused a stain to occur, or what would be the best remedy, contact a local service company before proceeding.

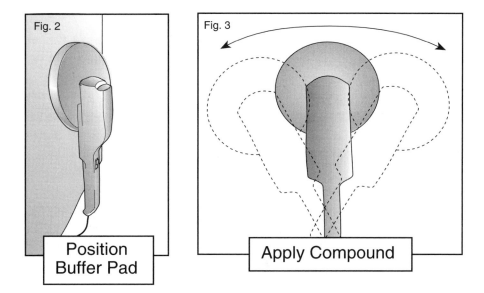

Fig. 2

Position
Buffer Pad

Fig. 3

Apply Compound

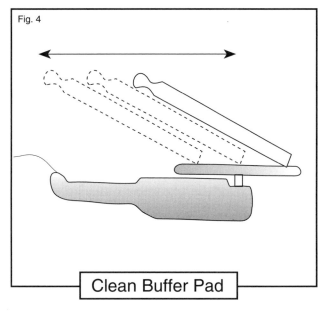

Fig. 4

Clean Buffer Pad

To begin the compounding phase, place the buffer pad as flat to the hull as possible before turning on the buffer (Fig. 2). This will prevent the polishing material from being thrown onto areas that are not to be polished such as the non-skid or exterior wood. With the buffer set to a low speed, spread the compound over an area approximately two feet square, using a side-to-side motion (Fig. 3). When the buffing pad becomes clogged with oxidation, hold the end of the paint stirring stick against the pad. While the pad is rotating, move the stick back and forth several times from the center to the edge to clear debris off the pad (Fig. 4).

This process is repeated as many times as needed until the entire boat has been compounded. Be certain to work the compound while it is damp; if allowed to dry prematurely, the compound material is difficult to use, and will not produce the best result.

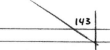

Of all the cautions I might offer, there are two that must be noted above all others:

1. Caution: Do not place too much pressure on the rotating buffer pad. If more than moderate pressure is brought to bear, the result will be damage to the gelcoat. This damage, referred to as "burning," is the complete removal of the gelcoat. If this occurs, the fiberglass will be plainly visible and the only remedy is to have a specialist repair the gelcoat, or paint the area. As you might guess, this repair could be far more costly than hiring a skilled professional to do the polishing work for you.

2. Caution: Be very aware of the buffer's electric cord and the cord's location relative to the buffer. It is easy to tangle the cord on the spinning buffer pad and, if this occurs, it will IMMEDIATELY result in damage to the buffer, damage to the boat or injury to you. If the cord is snagged by the buffer pad, the consequences will be instantaneous.

Once the hull has been compounded, it is time to apply the wax and complete the work with a final polish. For this phase, no machine is used. The general consensus at most service companies is that an electric buffer is to be used only for compounding, and not for wax application. The thinking here is that wax should represent a final finish and, except for a light final buff, an electric buffer should be unnecessary if the surface has been prepared properly to this point.

Apply the wax by placing a small quantity of paste or liquid wax on a clean cloth (Fig.5), and rubbing it onto an area about two feet square. With a circular motion, spread the wax evenly (Fig. 6). The wax should cover the surface, of course, but it should be a very thin layer of material.

Immediately, use a second cloth to remove any excess wax from the surface of the fiberglass; this time, use an up-and-down motion (Fig. 7). This difference of motion in

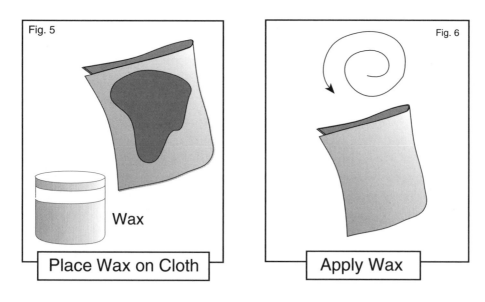

Fig. 5 — Place Wax on Cloth

Fig. 6 — Apply Wax

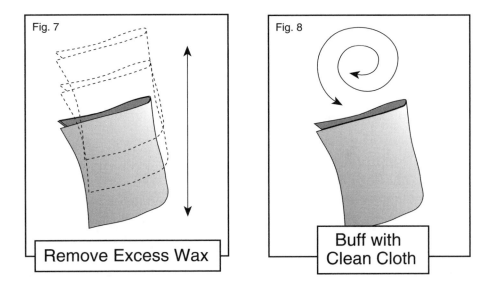

Fig. 7 — **Remove Excess Wax**

Fig. 8 — **Buff with Clean Cloth**

using the cloth will not only remove excess wax, but will also guarantee that any small areas missed in the original application will be covered.

Allow the wax to dry to a powder and then, using a rough cloth such as a terrycloth towel, remove the wax from the surface using a circular motion (Fig.8). As previously mentioned, use an electric buffer for a light polishing, then add the final touch of a cloth diaper used in a circular fashion. When complete, the surface should appear to be smooth, continuous and shining.

As with any well-done polishing job, water should bead up on the surface, and most stains should easily wash off for a period of four to six months. When the surface seems to get dirty more readily, or water ceases to bead on the surface, it is time to polish the fiberglass once again. If the work was done correctly last time, and the gelcoat is in generally good condition, only a good wax and polish should be required to restore the shine.

One final point. The smooth areas of fiberglass on deck and in the cockpit are polished in the same fashion as the hull, with one important difference — an electric buffer is not used even if compounding is required. The reason for this is the danger presented by the large number of small details on deck. The high-speed rotation of a buffer pad can cause damage to trim, get entangled in lines, or jump from your hands if the pad snags a block or other hardware. It may require more effort to polish the deck completely by hand, but the result should still be excellent and worth the extra effort.

Chapter Twenty-two
Wood Refinishing with Cetol

It used to be that sailing ships were built exclusively of wood, and were then painted in subdued colors that were utilitarian, but uninspired. Typical colors for most vessels of the 1800's would have been grays, blacks and earth tones. Often, the only bright colors seen on board were those of the flags that were flown from various locations in the rigging.

To break up this monochromatic color scheme, deckhouses, handrails and other trims on deck were constructed of teak, mahogany, ash or oak, and then coated with varnish instead of paint. Compared to the rest of the ship, these structures stood out in stark contrast with glossy surfaces that reflected the sun. Given this perspective, it is easy to understand how the term "brightwork" came into general use to describe the appearance of unpainted wood that was given a shiny protective finish.

On modern sailboats, very little remains of exterior wood due to the desire of many boat owners and designers for a "wash and go" vessel built of fiberglass and stainless steel. In truth the time, effort and skill required to maintain varnished surfaces are more than most skippers wish to deal with.

In times past, commercial sailing vessels would have had a full-time crew with little to do for months at sea other than maintain the ship. In fact, there was precious little maintenance ever done while in port. In contrast, pleasure boats are typically maintained by a crew of one or two who perform all maintenance when the boat is at the dock. And the chore that is nearly always lowest on the list of priorities is brightwork, a task almost universally postponed for as long as possible.

For older boats, extensive exterior wood surfaces still present a maintenance decision — varnish the wood every five or six months, oil the wood every couple of months, or ignore the issue entirely and expect to replace it eventually. In the meantime, unprotected teak will turn gray in color and eventually split, while ill-maintained varnished teak will crack and chip, and is viewed by most as unattractive.

If wood is finished and the finish is maintained properly at regular intervals, the wood should never need replacing, except for damage. Personally, I believe cosmetic appearance is important, so the option to do nothing is unacceptable.

TIP

Teak contains a natural oil, and is therefore somewhat self-preserving. Eventually, though, sun and weather take their toll.

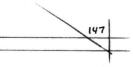

Let's assume that you have elected to do something with the wood on deck, so now your next decision is...what? For the traditionalist, there is varnish. For many skippers, merely the thought of varnishing sends chills up the spine. The fact is that excellent results with varnish can only be achieved with practice. And, as I am sure you know, the opportunities for practice occur more far more often than most of us would like. In addition to the practice required for good results, the expense can be somewhat oppressive — varnish will not keep well for long periods of time; the best brushes are expensive, and the clean-up is unpleasant.

Using a good-quality teak oil instead of varnish gets the job done quickly, but the results are a far cry from the appearance of finished woods. Oil will help to preserve the wood, but the color of the teak will darken significantly for a time before returning to the familiar gray color of unfinished wood. Further, in its prime state — sanded and unfinished — teak has a wonderful golden color that oil will never bring out.

There are many other options, including acrylic dressings, sealants and paint. In fact, there are dozens of different products that claim ease of use, beauty and longevity.

Suppose you want to do something, but oiling the wood isn't enough protection and varnish is too much work. What now? Well, what if there were a material that could protect fine exterior woods as well as varnish and required the same wood preparation as varnish, but was simpler to apply and required renewal only every year or two instead of every five or six months? Would you reconsider the idea of finishing your boat's exterior teak instead of applying an oil or, worse, doing nothing at all? If you answered "yes," you are among a growing number of boat owners who are improving the appearance of their boats with a product called Cetol from Akzo Coatings, Inc.

Cetol protects wood with a long-lasting finish that contains a very effective ultraviolet filter and a slightly warm tone of its own that most people find quite pleasing. Cetol is supplied in two parts — a base called Cetol Marine and a high gloss called Cetol Gloss. The base can be used, without the gloss, for a satin finish that will last about twelve months before renewal is needed. If the gloss is used as a topcoat for the base, the teak can be maintenance-free for two years.

Cetol has grown in popularity because it is easy to apply, subsequent renewals are relatively quick, and the interval between renewal coats is extremely long. No doubt there are other products available that are similar to Cetol and probably worth considering, but this discussion will be limited only to this product. *Note: Normally, I do not endorse any specific product, but Cetol is such a viable alternative to varnish that it begs to be treated as a special case.* Let's first identify the areas on deck that can benefit from refinishing.

On a sailboat that is a few years old (pre-1990), there are likely to be many opportunities for wood refinishing. As illustrated in Figure 1, typical teak items on the exterior of a sailboat can include grab rails, companionway hatch boards, hatch runners and other surrounding trim, coaming caps, cap rails, traveler bases, to name a few. Smaller items might include a base for a compass or winch, a mount for an instrument display, a halyard board, etc.; the list is potentially very long. But, regardless of the specific item, the same procedure of preparation is required in order to assure that the

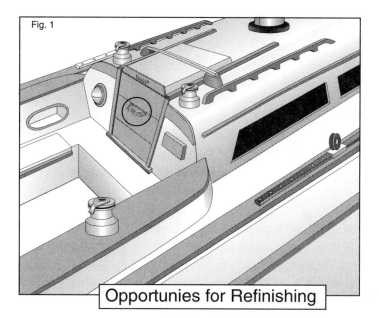

Opportunies for Refinishing

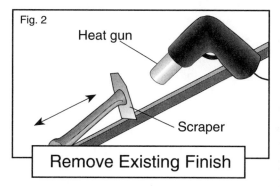

Remove Existing Finish

finish will be something to be proud of.

To begin, the finish that is currently on the wood must be removed. If the wood has only been oiled, there will be no finish to remove. However, the last application of oil should have been no more recent than ninety days. If this is not the case, it is probable that the new finish will separate from the wood within a short period of time. A drying-out period must be provided for oiled wood prior to initiating any resurfacing regardless of the choice.

If there is varnish or some other finish present, it must be completely removed before sanding or any further preparation can proceed. A heat gun (Fig. 2) combined with a scraper is the most commonly used tool to remove old finishes. A varnished surface can be removed by sanding, but it is far more difficult and, ultimately, more time-consuming than using a heat gun to soften the old finish.

Hold the heat gun a few inches away from the surface for only a moment or two. The idea is to warm the old finish so that it will easily separate from the wood. If you linger too long at one spot, you risk charring the wood. This will result in additional sanding and, if extensive, will detract from the wood's finished appearance. Move the scraper perpendicular to the blade; it should require very little time to become adept at the technique.

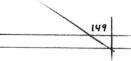

Caution: A heat gun can operate at temperatures of up to 2200 degrees, and the potential for damage or injury is great. It would be prudent to practice on something other than your boat.

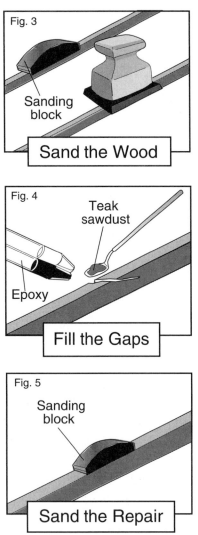

Fig. 3

Sanding block

Sand the Wood

Fig. 4

Teak sawdust

Epoxy

Fill the Gaps

Fig. 5

Sanding block

Sand the Repair

An alternative to using a heat gun is a liquid stripper. This product is brushed or wiped on, then removed with a putty knife or cloth. Liquid strippers are solvents and, as such, have the potential for damage if not carefully applied. Judicious use of a liquid stripper, however, is often the best option for small details such as carvings or wooden nameboards. *Note: When using a liquid stripper, wear protective gloves and avoid any contact with your skin, clothing, the gelcoat or even a painted surface. Liquid stripper will damage all of these surfaces.*

Once the old finish has been removed, the next step is to sand the surfaces of the wood (Fig. 3). A palm sander or random orbital sander will make short work of this phase of the preparation. For sensitive or small areas, a sanding block works well, albeit more slowly. In either case, a grit of 80 to 120 will take the surface down, eliminating minor cuts and gouges along the way. For final sanding, I recommend a grit of 180 or 220 to produce a fine, smooth surface. And if all of this sounds like a lot of work, that's because it is! *Note: Be certain to move the sanding block in the same direction as the grain of the wood; otherwise you will spend a lot of time trying to remove sanding marks later.*

If the wood has never been finished, the grain can often be very deep. For this reason, a three-phase sanding may be required, beginning with a 40 grit sandpaper. The 40 grit will leave marks behind, so it must be followed with an 80 or 120 grit, then finally 180 or 220 grit for the final sanding.

If there are small cracks or splits in the wood, the time to repair these is between the first and second sanding. A mix of sawdust and epoxy (Fig. 4) is the best filler for this type of repair. Prior to filling in the gaps, be certain to clean the repair area with acetone or a similar solvent in order to remove any surface oils that would prevent a good bond. After the mixture has had time to cure, sand the

TIP:

If the boat is scheduled to be polished about the same time as the wood refinishing, it is best to do the polishing first in order to provide the cleanest, smoothest possible surface for the masking tape.

repaired area with 120 grit sandpaper on a sanding block (Fig. 5), blending it into the surrounding surface.

If wood plugs need to be replaced, this is the time to tackle this job, too. If the plugs are not located in a high-stress or traffic area, it is wise to install the plugs with silicone or a similar sealant instead of using epoxy. (When it's time to replace the fasteners beneath the plugs, the task will be easy when compared to the difficulty of digging out plugs that have been inserted with epoxy.)

Only after all repairs have been made is it time to sand for the final time using a fine 180 or 220 grit sandpaper. If you are sanding cap rails or handrails, be sure to sand all the way around the curved edge to the underside of the wood. It is not customary to prep the entire underside of rubrails or handrails, but it is not uncommon either. In either case, the idea is to be certain that no rough edges can be felt when your hand is run the length of the wood. *Note: To avoid damaging the gelcoat with sandpaper, a scrap of laminate from a wood shop or lumberyard can act as an effective guard. Hold the laminate on the surface of the gelcoat while pressing the edge of the laminate firmly against the wood.*

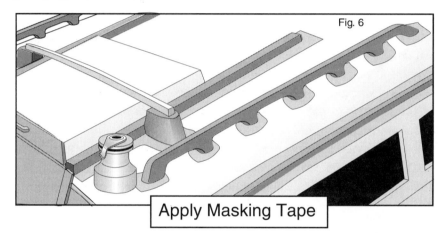

Fig. 6

Apply Masking Tape

After all of the sanding is complete, it is a good idea to rinse off the entire boat. This not only removes the vast majority of sawdust from the wood surfaces, but also cleans the deck to help prevent blowing dust from ruining the result. After everything has dried, the next step is to protect the fiberglass surfaces that are adjacent to the wood.

Although applying masking tape to protect the fiberglass (Fig. 6) is a time-consuming activity, it pays big dividends during the cleanup phase. You don't have to do this, but the project will look much more professional if the edges of the finished wood match the wood itself with no overlap onto caulking or the surrounding deck. Some people prefer to skip this step because of the amount of time it takes, but the elimination of this task is almost always evident in the finished results.

The masking tape used for this purpose is of a particular type called "Long-Mask," reviewed briefly in Chapter Two. It is a low-tack masking tape that is designed to be left in place for three days (green) to seven days (blue), even in the heat of summer. The tape sticks very well to clean, dry, smooth surfaces, and will leave a sharp line behind with no sticky residue.

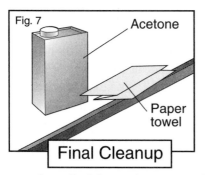

Final Cleanup

While applying the tape, take your time and line it up to the edges of the wood as closely as possible. You will find that many short pieces of tape will be required to accurately protect curves such as those around the attachment points of grab rails. If the sealant can be seen, it is preferable to mask this also, leaving only the surface of the wood to receive a protective finish.

When all of the masking is complete, the final step in the preparation phase is to remove any surface grit (Fig. 7); anything remaining on the surface of the wood will ruin the finish. A small vacuum cleaner, such as a wet/dry vac with a brush attachment, is helpful for removing surface debris prior to a final cleanup.

This final cleanup is best accomplished with acetone or a similar solvent, and disposable towels such as the type of paper towels found in a "Z-fold" dispenser. These are generally available from a janitorial supply house, and will leave behind fewer snags and lint than standard household paper towels.

Change towels often; it is not unusual for an entire stack of paper towels to disappear while preparing to refinish the wood on a typical 35 foot sailboat. The solvent will evaporate quickly, so the first of several coats of Cetol can be applied immediately after cleaning. *Note: If a cleaning solvent is not used, it is likely that no finishing material will adhere properly to the surface of the teak. This will invariably result in poor appearance, a shortened period of protection, or both.*

Before applying each coat of Cetol, be certain the liquid is well mixed, but allow it time to settle so air bubbles can rise to the surface; this should only take a few minutes. According to the manufacturer, Cetol should not be applied if the temperature is below

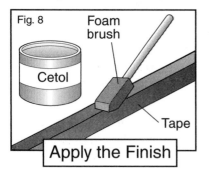

Apply the Finish

50 degrees or above 90 degrees Fahrenheit. In practice, however, I have found that a temperature as low as 45 degrees or as high as 100 degrees is workable, but who wants to be crawling around on deck doing anything in temperatures like that?

One of the many advantages of choosing Cetol instead of varnish is the use of foam brushes for application of the satin finish Marine base. Foam brushes are inexpensive, create a smooth finish and, most importantly, are disposable. When applying each coat, saturate no more than the lower half of the foam brush, remove the excess and then apply it to the wood in long, slow strokes (Fig. 8). If you move the brush too quickly along the surface of the wood, small air bubbles will result; go over the area again more slowly if this occurs. Ideally, the first of three coats is applied as thinly as possible with just enough liquid to cover the surface. Allow this first coat to dry for at least 24 hours.

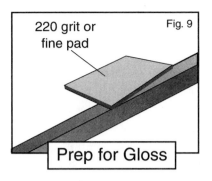

220 grit or fine pad

Fig. 9

Prep for Gloss

Another attraction for using this material instead of varnish is the fact that no sanding is required between coats of Cetol Marine, the base material. In fact, the instructions specifically state that sanding between coats is not recommended for exterior applications! Yessss!

The second and third coats are also applied at 24 hour intervals, but these are progressively heavier coats. In fact, the third coat should be as heavy as possible while still avoiding drips, runs and sags. After the third coat of Cetol, and another 24 hours have elapsed, the optional gloss coats can follow.

Cetol Marine dries to a hard satin finish that, in many instances, looks so good that no further finishing is desired. However, many owners prefer continuing this process by adding the gloss because it extends the time between renewals to two years while, at the same time, approximating the high shine of varnish. The gloss topcoat can be applied immediately after the third coat or it can be applied weeks, or even months, later. If you do elect to use the gloss, some additional preparation is required. *Note: The longer you delay between the third coat of satin and the first coat of gloss, the greater the chance that yet another coat of satin will be required in order to provide an unspoiled base for the gloss coats. This consideration is more cosmetic than functional, but isn't appearance the primary reason for refinishing?*

Before starting the first of two gloss coats, a fine-grit sandpaper (220 grit) or fine 3M Scotch Brite pad (Fig. 9) should be used to roughen the surface for better adhesion of the first gloss coat. There is a danger that too much of the Cetol will be removed while preparing for the gloss application, so great care and only a light pressure are needed. After the entire surface has been prepared appropriately, a vacuum and acetone should once again be used to make sure the surface is free of all debris before proceeding.

The application of the gloss is similar to the application of varnish in that a good quality Badger brush should be used. (A foam brush will work, but the results will be inferior.) "Badger" is the brand name of the best-known maker of fine brushes. These professional-quality brushes are made with natural fibers such as horse hair instead of synthetic fibers, and require extra care when they are used, cleaned or stored. For apply-

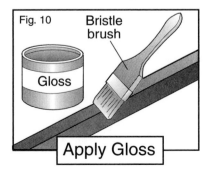

Fig. 10

Bristle brush

Gloss

Apply Gloss

ing finishes on a boat, a one-inch brush will handle most jobs; for large areas such as coaming caps or dorade boxes, a two-inch brush is worth considering. If handled properly, this type of brush will last for years and will produce the smoothest finish possible regardless of the material being applied.

Mix the liquid well, allow the bubbles to settle, then begin by using slow, long strokes

working from wet to dry (Fig. 10). The flow of gloss should follow the grain of the wood and be just enough to cover the surface.

After the first coat has had at least 48 hours to cure, use fine sandpaper or a fine Scotch Brite pad once more, followed by another cleaning with a solvent. The surface should now be very smooth, and ready for the final coat of gloss.

Like before, use only enough finish to just cover the surface; follow the grain of the wood and use long, slow strokes. Allow everything at least another day to cure.

To finish the project, remove the tape and use a solvent to clean any overlap on the fiberglass. If lightly discolored areas of accidental brush strokes on the fiberglass still remain even after acetone has been used, a polishing compound followed by a good marine wax should restore the appearance of smooth gelcoat.

Well, that's the whole process. You may be surprised to find that wood refinishing can be the most satisfying skill that you have ever tried to master. Of course, you may also discover it to be an excessive exercise in patience and attention to detail. But look at it this way: You won't have to do this again for another year or two!

Chapter Twenty-three
Insulating the Engine Compartment

Boats are great places to relax on a beautiful balmy evening, especially at anchor...the lapping of the water against the hull, a gentle breeze that rocks you to sleep and the cozy feeling of being aboard. It can make you feel as if all the expense and effort that go into owning a boat have been amply rewarded. In fact, you might even find yourself feeling a bit sorry for those who just can't seem to understand why it is we are so intense about being on the water. Ha, paradise!

Until, that is, someone starts an engine or a generator. Noise travels so quickly and unobstructed across the water it can sometimes make you feel as though the noise has been aimed specifically at you! But did you ever stop to wonder this: If the racket seems that loud to you, how loud must it seem to the people aboard *that other boat*? You probably couldn't care less about the other crew; after all, they came aboard their boat knowing the noise problem existed. But the effect of the problem remains the same: The noise is very disturbing, extremely unwelcome and, for the most part, avoidable.

Even on board your own boat there are likely to be several places where noise could be reduced to more pleasant levels. The engine and genset are obvious examples, but how about a noisy battery charger, fresh water pump or air conditioning compressor? Skippers on other boats may not be able to hear some of this equipment operate, but no doubt you do. And the area that is likely to have the most objectionable sound level is the engine compartment.

If your sailboat is equipped with a gasoline engine, the noise level is often not an issue; after all, gasoline engines were originally intended for use in automobiles and noise reduction was a part of the design. But most sailboats have diesel engines and diesels were never meant for quiet operation; the ancestry of most diesel motors can be traced back to tractors and construction equipment.

If your boat is in the 28- to 42-foot range, it is undoubtedly equipped with a diesel engine. On these boats, the engine area is not so much an "engine room" as it is an enclosed space. The dimensions of this space are typically small — three or four feet on a side — and the placement is invariably below the cockpit and near the galley, or adjacent to the main salon. Since all of these locations are areas in which we spend a great deal of time, it is more for our own comfort than our neighbors' comfort that noise reduction should be addressed and resolved.

The material available for accomplishing sound reduction is typically a sheet of a

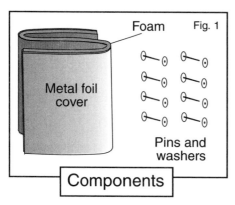

Foam | Fig. 1

Metal foil cover

Pins and washers

Components

metallic or Mylar base to which a one-inch layer of foam has been attached (Fig. 1). In times past, a layer of lead was sandwiched between the metal base and the foam to help absorb sound. Today, a high-density polymer is used instead. Normally sold in a sheet measuring 3½' by 4½', this material can be cut with either shears or a utility knife. Two methods are available to hold this foam liner in place: contact cement or metal pins that have a large flat base and a long shank, and are glued to the interior walls of the compartment.

In either case, the installation process is simple. Mark and cut the foam (Fig. 2) to fit one or more adjacent walls of the enclosed space. And, as always, measure twice and cut once. For any fixtures attached to the

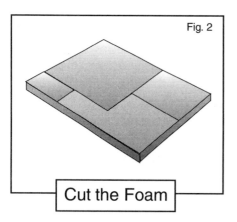

Fig. 2

Cut the Foam

walls, make cutouts by creating an opening in the foam; alternately, these items may be removed and reattached after the foam has been set into place. *Note: The metallic side of the foam must face the interior of the compartment. If you draw the cutout marks on the foam side, as opposed to the foil side, you must remember to lay out the sections in reverse of the final installation.*

If you are using pins, fasten them with epoxy to at least seven places on each wall of the enclosure (Fig. 3). Epoxy requires as little as a few hours to cure but, if possible, it would be best to leave it undisturbed overnight. After the adhesive has had time to cure, the foam is marked on its reverse side to indicate the location of the pins. Cut a small "X" at these spots and then, with the

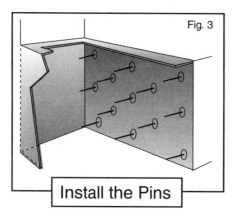

Fig. 3

Install the Pins

metallic side towards you, press the foam into place on the pins (Fig. 4). Slide the washers onto the pins as far they will go, then cut off the excess pin length, leaving about ½" protruding above the washer. The only potential difficulty in the process is getting the foam into place; since it's rather heavy, you may encounter some handling difficulties.

If you have chosen to use contact cement instead of pins, all surfaces to be glued must be coated with adhesive (Fig. 5). The cement can be applied somewhat sparingly to the fiberglass surfaces, but must be heavy on the foam due to some absorption of the adhesive. You may find an inexpensive disposable brush or small roller handy for applying the contact cement. *Note: Contact cement MUST be used in a well-ventilated area. For this reason, I strongly recommended that this project be done, to the extent possible, somewhere other than the cabin of the boat if the engine covers are removable.*

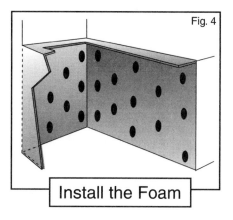

Install the Foam

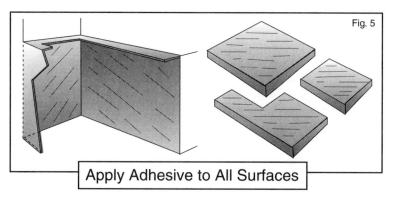

Apply Adhesive to All Surfaces

After the contact cement has had about an hour to completely dry, press the sections of foam into place (Fig. 6). Be certain to align the sections carefully; once the adhesive-coated surfaces touch, it is difficult to remove and reposition the foam.

Regardless of the installation method, there are likely to be small gaps along the engine covers of most boats. Seal these small, narrow areas by using readily available, adhesive-backed weatherstripping. It may be necessary to use a double layer of weatherstripping to fill gaps around the edges of an engine cover.

Other applications

Although metallic-backed foam insulation is primarily intended for use as a covering for the interior walls of an engine enclosure, it works equally well to dampen annoying sounds from other devices on board. If you have a noisy air conditioning or refrigeration compressor, for example, an easily made cover will silence this item permanently.

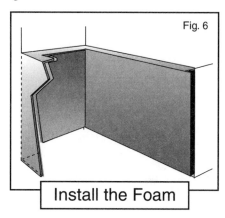

Install the Foam

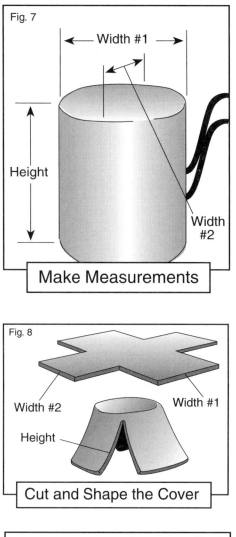

Make Measurements

Cut and Shape the Cover

Install the Cover

To make an acoustic cover for a compressor, measure its height and width; the width of the compressor may not be the same on all sides (Fig. 7). After noting the dimensions, lay out a "plus sign" (Fig. 8), and cut it out. It is quite common to find that two sides of the "plus sign" are of one dimension, and two are of another.

Once the cutout is complete, fold down the insulating foam over the compressor. Be certain to keep the foil side to the OUTSIDE of the cover. *Note: This orientation is the opposite of what was done to the inside of the engine compartment. If you place the metallic layer on the inside of the acoustic cover, heat as well as noise will be reflected back to the compressor. This build-up of heat could result in premature failure of the compressor.*

After shaping the cover to the compressor, use very long nylon tie wraps or a light nylon line to bind the cover to the compressor (Fig. 9). If the cover is made correctly, the edges of it should meet when the fasteners are tightened, completely enclosing the unit. This same technique can be applied to silence a noisy fresh water pump or any other device that does not require ambient air cooling for its operation.

When compared to the high degree of reduced noise and heat from the engine, this project is nominal in cost for the benefits it provides. Perhaps best of all, it requires only a few hours to complete.

Chapter Twenty-four
An Opening Port in a Window

If your boat is like most, the galley is located just inside the companionway. This is a good arrangement for many reasons, not the least of which is ventilation. But even though the stove may be placed near the companionway, it is not directly beneath it. The result is that odors cling to the overhead because there is no opening directly over the cooking area; on occasion, steam can completely fill the main cabin.

A fan in the galley can go a long way towards providing some relief from trapped cooking fumes, but the best solution would be to vent the odors out of the saloon by way of a hatch or port. It is interesting to note that an opening port or hatch in the galley is missing from most boats under about forty feet, even though vessels in this size range are in the most need of such a feature.

If you choose to install a deck hatch, the size most commonly used is about eight inches square, and is typically located as much as possible directly over the stove. Although installing a deck hatch is an excellent solution, it is a less attractive option than a port for three reasons:

- The hole to be cut is much larger than would be required for a port.
- It can affect deck integrity and strength.
- It may not be useable in inclement conditions.

An opening port, on the other hand, is more appealing because it addresses all three of these issues and offers a simpler installation. Often, the boatbuilder can still supply an opening port that matches the original equipment even though many years have passed since the boat was produced. If the builder is out of business, a matching port can often be sourced directly from the manufacturer through a local marine supplier. *Note: It is often more expedient to contact the manufacturer directly if the likelihood exists that a component may have been discontinued, updated or issued a different part number. Armed with this information, the part can then be purchased through a local retailer.*

If you look at other people's boats as much as I do, you have probably seen solar-powered mushroom-shaped vents installed into the lens of deck hatches. When an opening port is installed into a cabin window — the most common location — the procedure is similar. In fact, this project will also draw upon the many of the techniques discussed in Chapter Seven: Relocating a VHF Radio.

To begin, locate the window on the cabin side that is nearest the stove. It is critical to measure this window from inside the cabin; the area available for a port is smaller

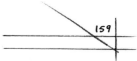

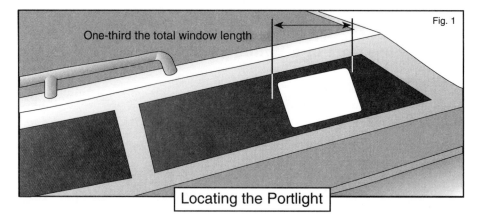

One-third the total window length

Fig. 1

Locating the Portlight

than the exterior opening would appear. Leaving several inches of the window to surround the port will result in the most secure installation. In addition, aesthetics suggest that the port should be installed about one-third the distance from either end of the window (Fig. 1).

After you have decided upon the location, cover the area with masking tape; this will protect the window and provide a surface on which to draw. But instead of using common beige masking tape, purchase (or borrow) a roll of blue or green 3M Long-Mask masking tape that is normally used in conjunction with brightwork refinishing.

In order to minimize the potential mess inside the cabin, tape a large plastic storage bag or small trash bag to the inside of the window. Position the bag so the opening completely encircles the hole to be cut. (This simple precaution will eliminate almost all of the cleanup required in the cabin!)

Mark the outline of the opening to be cut by holding the port in place on the window and tracing around it. Mark the centers of four ½" inch holes, one in each corner of the cutout (Fig. 2). The actual cutout should be no more than ⅛" larger than the port's opening. Using a drill set to a slow speed, bore a ½" hole in each corner, being careful not to exceed the outline. After the holes have been made, insert the blade of the jigsaw into any of the holes and cut out the opening using a slow speed. For this task, if you choose a blade made specifically for fiberglass, the edge will be fine, and chipping around the opening will not be a worry. After the opening has been cut, a few passes of a medium file will render the raw edge less sharp.

Next, insert the exterior plate of the port into the cutout, and mark the position of the screws. For proper alignment of the exterior plate and to provide a good weather seal, be very careful to accurately mark and drill the holes for fasteners. Drill all of the holes, then remove the masking tape from the outside of the window and the plastic bag from the inside.

TIP:

Long-Mask is a low tack masking tape that is easily removed without leaving a gummy residue behind. This is significant when you recognize that many of the chemicals and solvents used for adhesive removal will fog Lexan, Plexiglas and acrylic.

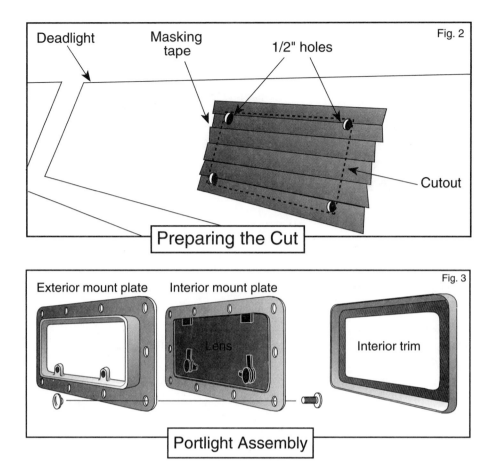

Fig. 2

Deadlight   Masking tape   1/2" holes   Cutout

Preparing the Cut

Fig. 3

Exterior mount plate   Interior mount plate   Lens   Interior trim

Portlight Assembly

The only step yet to do is the assembly (Fig. 3). If the window and port are smoked or dark plastic, using black 3M5200, black Life-Seal from Boat-Life, or a similar black adhesive-sealant is recommended in order to enhance the appearance of the installation. If the opening port has an aluminum exterior frame, a better choice might be a clear adhesive-sealant. Be generous enough with the sealant so that a small amount of it will ooze out around all the edges of the plate surrounding the port. Prior to curing, any excess sealant can be cleaned away with a damp paper towel. *Note: Instead of cleaning away excess adhesive-sealant with a damp cloth before it has cured, an alternative is to allow the bead of sealant around the edges of the port to cure completely. The excess can then be removed using a small razor knife such as an Xacto knife.* Under NO circumstances should you use

TIP:

A bi-metal jigsaw blade is a useful alternative to a blade made only for fiberglass. A bi-metal blade is a general-purpose blade, available with either 24 or 32 teeth per inch, that will create a very clean edge when sawing into fiberglass, metal and plastics.

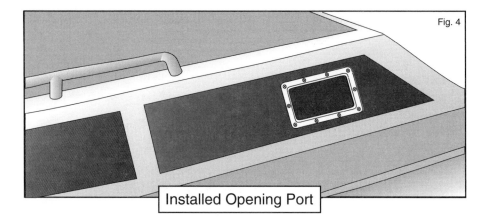

Fig. 4

Installed Opening Port

acetone, 3M Adhesive Remover or a similar product on plastic ports or windows due to a resulting fog that can only be remedied by buffing the plastic.

Place the exterior trim plate over the cutout, and attach it to the interior section with fasteners that will also pass through holes in the window. Tighten the screws securely, and allow about 24 hours for the sealant to cure completely. *Note: Do not over-tighten the screws. If this occurs, most plastics will crack or split; at worst, the fasteners will pull all the way through the material.*

If done correctly, the opening port should not leak and will appear (Fig. 4) to have been supplied as original equipment from the builder. If there is a single key to the success of this upgrade, it is generous but controlled application of adhesive-sealant.

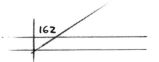

Chapter Twenty-five
Dockside Water Connection

Whether you live aboard or weekend cruise, whether your boat is power or sail, and regardless of the boat size or water tankage, an inescapable routine chore is the filling of fresh water tanks. Luckily, there is a way to avoid this task and provide a virtually unlimited supply of fresh water, at least while at the dock. You can accomplish this through the installation of a dockside faucet hook-up that plumbs directly into the boat's fresh water system. What's more, depending upon how far you are willing to go, the system can even fill your water tanks without messing about with hoses.

This project is simple in concept, but requires a substantial amount of time to complete. The cost is not onerous if you provide your own labor — you CAN do it — but some skippers get queasy at the thought of altering major systems such as the plumbing and DC electrical configurations.

If you would like to have access to city water service while on board, but don't have the time or inclination to take on this project, read on so you will know what to look for in a proper installation. But if you are ready to get your hands wet, you will undoubtedly be proud of the results.

To begin, recognize that this project has three parts: 1) the connection at the dock, 2) the connection on the boat and, 3) the connection to the existing system. Let's begin with the connection at the dock.

On the dock

As illustrated in Figure 1, the dockside connection is comprised of a high-capacity, in-line water filter attached to the faucet, with a length of garden hose connected to the filter. The length of the hose can be whatever is necessary to reach the boat, but the hose itself should be only of the type that is specifically sold for use with drinking water. These hoses are always labeled as safe for supplying drinking water, and are usually recognizable by their white color with blue stripe.

To create as leak-proof a bond as possible, wrap Teflon plumber's tape around the male threads of the faucet and filter exit ports before screwing together the components. The next step is the faucet connection on the boat.

The fitting

Ideally, the water connection on board will be located in an area this is both out of the way of traffic and easy to access. Typically, the location most commonly chosen on

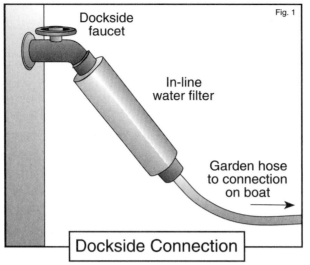

Dockside faucet

In-line water filter

Garden hose to connection on boat →

Dockside Connection

a sailboat is on or near the transom. Not only does this address both location requirements, but it also generally provides easier access to the boat's internal plumbing — especially if the vessel is equipped with a cockpit shower.

Once you have chosen the location, you will need to cut a one-inch (or larger) hole in the fiberglass to accommodate the faucet. The exact diameter of this opening will be determined by the brand and model of faucet that you choose. For this installation, the faucet you choose should have three important features:

- It should be made from stainless steel or chrome-plated brass with a garden hose thread on the exposed end, and a hose barb or garden hose thread on the interior end.
- It should have a screw-on cap with a chain and, optionally, a shut-off valve (Fig. 2). This may tend to make the entire fitting protrude further from the surface of the fiberglass than a connection without a shut-off valve, but it will also provide an extra margin of safety and convenience.

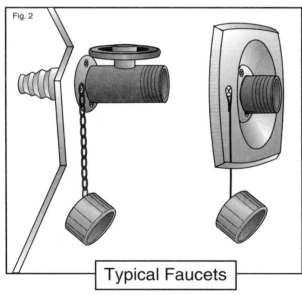

Typical Faucets

- It should have a pressure-reduction valve incorporated into the connection. *Note: If the fitting is not supplied with a pressure-reduction valve, a separate valve of this type MUST be added. Water from the faucet on the dock is supplied at 80-100 psi (pounds per square inch), while the pressure water system on a pleasure boat is typically 25-35 psi.*

The faucet should be bedded into the opening using an adhesive-sealant such as 3M's 5200 or Boat-Life Life-Seal, then allowed to cure for 48 hours before making the final connections.

The plumbing lines

The time-consuming part of this project involves the plumbing that must run from the fitting at the stern to a point just past the pressure water pump. The tubing connection from the interior end of the faucet can be either clear vinyl tubing, clear reinforced hose that is made specifically for drinking water applications, PVC pipe or copper. Of the options, I feel that the best combination of features lies with

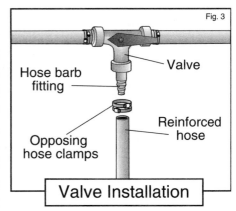

Fig. 3

Hose barb fitting

Valve

Reinforced hose

Opposing hose clamps

Valve Installation

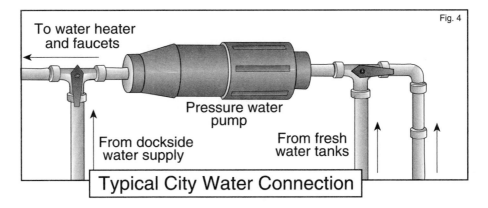

Fig. 4

To water heater and faucets

Pressure water pump

From dockside water supply

From fresh water tanks

Typical City Water Connection

⅝" or ¾" ID (inside diameter) reinforced hose. It is flexible, strong, mildew-resistant, reasonable in cost, and can be installed with standard barb fittings and stainless steel hose clamps. If your boat is less than ten years old, it is very likely that reinforced drinking water hose was used when the vessel was built.

Similarly, the valve that must be installed is available in many forms, but my choice would be an assembly made of plastic components, as opposed to brass or bronze, with barbed fittings on all three ends (Fig. 3).

I suggest you begin this part of the modification at the point where the new incoming line will meet the existing plumbing system, then work back to the fitting at the stern. Begin by shutting off all valves that supply water from the storage tanks to the pressure water pump; there should be a separate valve for each tank (Fig. 4). Turn on the cold water tap nearest the pump for just a moment or two, allowing the last of the water remaining in the pump and the lines to run through the system.

TIP:

A small scrap of laminate an inch or two wide can help protect existing water lines while enlarging an opening in a bulkhead.

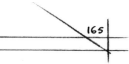

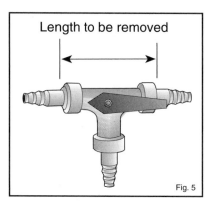

Length to be removed

Fig. 5

Locate a section of the existing tubing, near the pressure water pump, that can accommodate the valve you have chosen to install. Be certain that this section is long enough for the entire length of the valve, including the barbed ends. To determine how much of the existing tubing must be removed (Fig. 5), measure the distance between the ends of the new valve, but do NOT include the length of the barbed ends. Once you have determined this distance, you

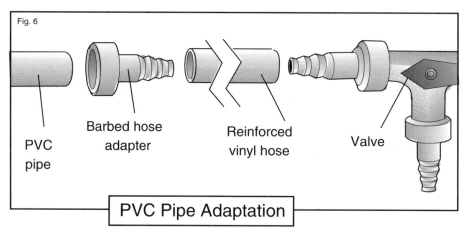

Fig. 6

PVC pipe

Barbed hose adapter

Reinforced vinyl hose

Valve

PVC Pipe Adaptation

are ready to cut the existing tubing. Place a small bucket below the point of the cut in order to catch as much water as possible that might still remain in the line. Then, with as straight a line as possible, cut the tubing with a sharp knife or a hacksaw. If your boat has PVC plumbing lines, a barbed hose fitting must be glued to the cut end of the pipe in order to use flexible tubing when installing a valve that also has barbed fittings. An inexpensive ratchet tool is available that can cut PVC pipe cleanly and straight, every time. Once the barbed fitting has been glued to the cut end of the PVC pipe, the valve can be installed using short sections of reinforced hose (Fig. 6).

Once the valve is in place, connect flexible hose on both sides of the valve and secure the hose in place with two hose clamps at each connection. Attach the incoming water line to the valve, double clamp it and then route the balance of the tubing aft through the boat to the general location of the fitting at the stern. *Note: Be certain that the valve is in the CLOSED position before proceeding. This valve will not be opened until other sections of the installation have been checked for leaks.*

Figure 7 is a typical plumbing plan that illustrates the location of existing water lines aboard a 32-foot sailboat. It is a good practice to follow these paths when running new or additional water lines in order to simplify the process. Of course, if you find alternative routes that appear to be easier to use, go for it. After all, the builder had the distinct advantage of laying the water lines prior to the boat's completion.

You undoubtedly will find that the existing water lines pass through one or more

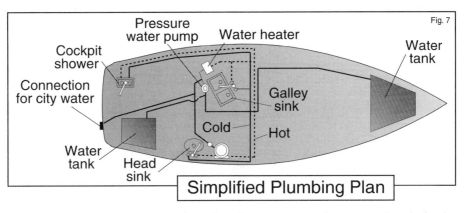

Fig. 7

Simplified Plumbing Plan

bulkheads; this is quite common, but often the openings are large enough only for the original hoses. Unless these existing holes can accommodate a new water line with room to spare, the opening(s) must be enlarged or other routes must be found.

Even if the new line will fit within an existing opening, be certain that there is ample space, otherwise the surrounding fiberglass will eventually chafe through the hose. If the dockside water source happens to be in use at a time when a water line chafes through, the boat will quickly fill with more water than an electric bilge pump can handle.

In the event that a bulkhead opening must be enlarged, the easiest method of doing so will often lie in the use of a keyhole saw. This manual saw has a blade that is about a foot in length, triangular in shape, and with a large handle designed for single hand operation. An electric alternative to a keyhole saw is a reciprocating saw. This tool has a blade that passes in and out of a guarded end, duplicating the back-and-forth motion of a manual saw. In either case, be very careful not to puncture the existing water lines.

After the vinyl hose has been routed through the boat to the stern, the final connection can be made. The interior end of the faucet will have the familiar barbed fitting over which the hose can be placed, followed by the customary double hose clamps.

Before turning on the water supply, take a few moments to recheck all of the connections. Once you are certain that all is as it should be, turn on the boat's pressure water supply and check for leaks. If all connections appear to be dry, turn off the ship's pressure water system and turn on the water supply at the dock. *Note: Do not turn on the water from the dock until you have verified that no leaks exist at any of the new connections.* If a leak develops or if a clamp comes loose when the system is first pressurized, the worse thing possible is an unlimited supply of water flowing into the boat.

If the connection to the boat also appears to be free of leaks, the next section can be checked. Open the valve on the fitting at the stern and open the new valve that you just installed. Check for leaks from the fitting at the stern to the valve near the pressure water pump. Since a portion of this segment is hidden, it is helpful to have at least one other person help with this part. If you discover leaks, turn off the water supply at the stern fitting, repair the leaks, and then try again. If a leak develops, it is almost always the result of hose clamps that are not sufficiently tight. Again, open the faucet at the stern and check for leaks. If none are found, your work is finished.

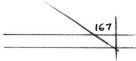

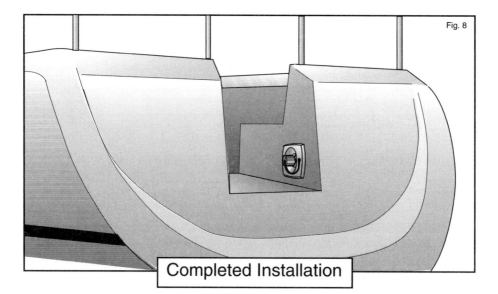

Fig. 8

Completed Installation

Congratulations! You have just made life much easier for yourself while at the dock.

Just think — unlimited showers, no weekly water tank fill, and no noise from a pressure pump. Of course, there is the problem of remembering to be conservative with water while under way when a limited water supply is once again a reality. Figure 8 illustrates an example of a city water connection located on the inside of a walk-through transom.

In closing, I offer a final thought. It would add little to the cost of this project to install a "T" connector near the galley on the new water line in order to provide a line to the head. If this additional water line is installed (along with a valve) to the hose attached to the through-hull that provides flush water to the toilet, you can enjoy the pleasure of using fresh water instead of raw water. Assuming that the holding tank is pumped out on a regular basis, this modification will result in the elimination of almost all of the odors from the head.

Fair winds!

Index